Series

of

Interviews on the

Subject

of

POLARIS

U. S. Naval Institute
Annapolis, Maryland

Preface

This volume contains transcripts of interviews on the concept and development of POLARIS as a weapons system of the U. S. Navy.

Included are the interviews with Vice Admiral Wm. F. Raborn, Jr., USN (Ret.); with Admiral Arleigh Burke, USN (Ret.), Chief of Naval Operations at the time; with the Hon. Thomas S. Gates, Secretary of the Navy; with Carleton Shugg, head of Electric Boat; with Dr. Jack Dunlop, Gordon Pehrson and Clement Hayes Watson - all close associates of Adm. Raborn in the initial efforts of the Special Project in the decade of the 1950s.

Other interviews on POLARIS are to be found in the individual Oral History volumes of the following: Vice Admiral J. B. Colwell, USN (Ret.), Deputy Director of SP under Adm. Raborn; Rear Admiral Robert H. Wertheim, USN (Ret.), the fourth officer to serve as Director of SP and a man associated with the project for its inception; John B. Buescher, Chief Engineer of SP from 1956 to 1981.

An index has not been provided for the interviews in this volume because they all focus on the project itself. As such, they constitute what amounts to a single reference.

John T. Mason, Jr.
Director of Oral History

May, 1982

TO WHOM IT MAY CONCERN:

The collection of oral interviews in the Naval Institute's volume on POLARIS contains two interviews that are without signed releases. They are the interviews with

        Dr. Jack Dunlop
            and
        Mr. Gordon Pehrson

Both of these men gladly gave me the interviews but neither one wanted to be bothered further with the interview or with corrections of the transcript. These interviews contain nothing of a restricted nature...both men merely contributing some factual evidence on the development of the POLARIS project under the aegis of Admiral Raborn. Mr. Pehrson in fact did not give me a special interview but only one at a time when he and I happened to be with Vice Admiral J. B. Colwell in the Washington apartment of the Admiral. Colwell invited Pehrson to participate at that time with him in making some comments on PERT and other aspects of the program as it developed in the first year of the venture.

When I prepared the POLARIS volume for the bindery I did not pursue the matter further with Mr. Pehrson because of his earlier statement that he did not want to be bothered. Dr. Dunlop is deceased.

                                    John T. Mason, Jr.
                                    (Former Director of Oral History
                                      at the U. S. Naval Institute)

                                    January 4, 1983.

DECLARATION OF TRUST

The undersigned does hereby appoint and designate as his (her) Trustee herein, the Secretary-Treasurer and Publisher of the United States Naval Institute to perform and discharge the following duties, powers, and privileges in connection with the possession and use of a certain taped interview between the undersigned and the Oral History Department of the United States Naval Institute.

1. Classification of Transcript.

(✓)a. If classified OPEN, the transcript(s) may be read or the recording(s) audited by the qualified personnel upon presentation of proper credentials, as determined by the Secretary-Treasurer of the U.S. Naval Institute.

( )b. If classified PERMISSION REQUIRED TO CITE OR QUOTE, the user will be required to obtain permission in writing from the interviewee prior to quoting or citing from either the transcript(s) or the recording(s).

( )c. If classified PERMISSION REQUIRED, permission must be obtained in writing from the interviewee before the transcribed interview(s) can be examined or the tape recording(s) audited.

( )d. If classified CLOSED, the transcribed interview(s) and the tape recording(s) will be sealed until a time specified by the interviewee. This may be until the death of the interviewee or for any specified number of years.

2. It is expressly understood that in giving this authorization, I am in no way precluded from placing such restrictions as I may desire upon use of the interview at any time during my lifetime, nor does this authorization in any way affect my rights to the copyright of my literary expressions that may be contained in the interview.

Witness my hand and seal this 12 day of September 1981

William F. Raborn Jr
VAdm USN (Ret.)

I hereby accept and consent to the foregoing Declaration of Trust and the powers therein conferred upon me as Trustee:

22 Sept 1981

DECLARATION OF TRUST

The undersigned does hereby appoint and designate as his (her) Trustee herein, the Secretary-Treasurer and Publisher of the United States Naval Institute to perform and discharge the following duties, powers, and privileges in connection with the possession and use of a certain taped interview between the undersigned and the Oral History Department of the United States Naval Institute.

1. Classification of Transcript.

   (✓)a. If classified OPEN, the transcript(s) may be read or the recording(s) audited by the qualified personnel upon presentation of proper credentials, as determined by the Secretary-Treasurer of the U. S. Naval Institute.

   (✓)b. If classified PERMISSION REQUIRED TO CITE OR QUOTE, the user will be required to obtain permission in writing from the interviewee prior to quoting or citing from either the transcript(s) or the recording(s).

   (✓)c. If classified PERMISSION REQUIRED, permission must be obtained in writing from the interviewee before the transcribed interview(s) can be examined or the tape recording(s) audited.

   (✓)d. If classified CLOSED, the transcribed interview(s) and the tape recording(s) will be sealed until a time specified by the interviewee. This may be until the death of the interviewee or for any specified number of years.

2. It is expressly understood that in giving this authorization, I am in no way precluded from placing such restrictions as I may desire upon use of the interview at any time during my lifetime, nor does this authorization in any way affect my rights to the copyright of my literary expressions that may be contained in the interview.

Witness my hand and seal this 1st day of Dec 1978

William F. Raborn Jr.

I hereby accept and consent to the foregoing Declaration of Trust and the powers therein conferred upon me as Trustee:

R. E. Bowker Jr.

Interview No. 1 with Vice Admiral William F. Raborn, Jr.,
U.S. Navy (Retired)

Place: His residence in Arlington, Virginia

Date: Friday morning, 15 September 1972

Subject: Polaris Project

By: John T. Mason, Jr.

Q: Admiral, I'm delighted that you've consented to do this story on Polaris. It comes from the horse's mouth, so to speak! I wonder if we shouldn't begin, however, with a bit of your own personal background in the Navy.

You were the man who had all the qualifications that seemed necessary to head up this Special Projects Division in the Navy. Both Admiral Burke and Admiral Sides were in agreement on that. How did you happen to acquire all of this necessary experience? How did you happen to have this in your background? Perhaps you might talk about this for a bit.

Adm. R.: That's a difficult subject to address because the evolution of a person's life is so markedly influenced by his associations and assignments to duty in the case of a military person. Some of the ingredients, I think, that were important in this kind of job, or, as a matter of fact, any kind of a job which requires dedicated effort are a basic enthusiasm for life, a great amount of personal energy, and a thorough appreciation that a person doesn't do everything by himself, and that the collective efforts of those that are around him have to be utilized and brought to bear in an optimum way on the problem at hand.

Going back a little bit in my own naval career, it was filled with great enthusiasm for sea duty and for the Navy life in particular. The motivation which I received at the hands of the officers in the Navy at that time was great. Obviously they should receive credit for the enthusiasm with which young officers like myself tackled their job and dedicated themselves to the Navy life. This is part and parcel of the word "leadership" which the Navy and the military in general prize so greatly. For example, in officers as well as enlisted men, the element of leadership is given top priority in the rating or effectiveness of a person. "Leadership" is known in civilian circles as the ability to manage and get things done, I believe.

Q: Some of that is part of one's natural endowment, some of it is acquired.

Adm. R.: I suppose that the combination of enthusiasm, energy, and dedication just makes a person a better leader. You dedicate yourself to your job, you learn more about it, you become enthused, you enthuse other people, you get other people to dedicate their efforts, and the result is you have a build-up of ongoing efforts which commanding officers or officers aboard ship show and result in a ship being a good ship, a ship that's smart, and in which people respond to their duties with pride, and they're alert. All of these things are bound up in the word "leadership."

My duties at sea were many and varied. They were principally in the ordnance end of the Navy, gunnery officer of ships and so forth. I did have some communications duty, which was collateral. But at an early age, five years after graduating from the Naval Academy, I entered flight training and became a naval aviator, and for the rest of my career in the Navy I was a naval aviator. I was a rated pilot until the day I retired in September 1963.

Q: Did your experience with aviation, perhaps, contribute to your later ability to make clear-cut and rapid decisions, which was a factor in your success with Polaris?

Adm. R.: I suppose that the qualities that made a good naval aviator undoubtedly encompassed many of the qualities of which you speak. Obviously, to fly a fighter plane - and I was a fighter pilot for a large number of years - you had to do things well, if you were going to live, and so that zeal for proficient flying became a guiding way of life for successful fighter pilots. So I emphasize that enthusiasm and the zest for living, is part and parcel of a good leader. The ability to make good decisions and live with it and live because of them were a part of our normal training. I never considered myself an outstanding officer, but I always felt that I could carry my part of the load. My training and duties in aviation squadrons had to do with gunnery. Gunnery fascinated me from the time I was a little child, guns of all kinds.

We found certain gunnery deficiencies in my duties in naval aviation squadrons. For example, it was my dream to teach people to shoot fixed machine guns from fighter planes better, also teach them to dive bomb better from planes. So I was sent to Pensacola as a fighter plane instructor for two years, which I throughly enjoyed. Then went to duty in long-range sea planes (patrol planes) about two years before the outbreak of World War II. Patrol planes, or flying boats, as they were called, were considerably short on ordnance equipment, ability to do offensive things. The planes were large and could carry tremendous weights, yet we had no aviation torpedoes, we had no way to carry torpedoes aboard the planes. Obviously, these planes could range out thousands of miles from the base and could very well come upon an enemy vessel in time of war and, if they had torpedoes aboard, they could perhaps sink or cripple the ship.

We had no aviation depth bombs to use against submarines, enemy submarines in time of war. We had no way to carry them. We did have bomb racks, one on each wing. So I took it on myself with the cooperation of people in other parts of the Navy locally in San Diego, to adapt surface-ship torpedoes so that they could be carried on the wings of patrol planes. The Torpedo Station prepared torpedoes for running and we fixed box fins on the tail to give it some aerodynamic qualities as they dropped from the patrol planes, and I myself flew the planes and did all the testing. I had another plane alongside to take pictures of it, and we were able to develop fins and altitudes and attitudes of the plane for dropping destroyer (ship) torpedoes successfully from patrol planes.

We sent in, I remember, an official report to the then Bureau of Ordnance along with pictures in sequence from the time the torpedo was dropped until it entered the water and, theoretically, hit the target, which was a destroyer, and we got a blistering letter back saying, you can't do that, these actions exceeded our authority, such things were not a matter for the fleet to experiment with, and this was not to be done! This was my first brush with intrenched bureaucracy!

Q: You were adequately cowed by that, I suspect!

Adm. R.: No, we were not. We just felt, well, no wonder we don't have aerial torpedoes for planes with that kind of attitude at the seat of the government.

Also, we had no depth bombs designed to be dropped from airplanes and we had no way to carry them, as I mentioned before. So, with the aid of metalsmiths, we concocted out of steel rods a device that fitted into the bomb racks which would carry a ship type depth bomb on each wing. These were destroyer depth bombs, 300-pound non streamlined babies. But we also took these out and dropped them very successfully. So we were rather smug about making ourselves in a makeshift way, prepared for battle against surface ships and submarines. As a matter of fact, our wing of patrol planes was deployed to Pearl Harbor at Kaneohe just 22 days before World War II broke out. When we got there the aviation admiral in charge of all the aviation units in Oahu looked at our innovations and said, "These must receive highest priority," and he ordered immediate manufacture on a round-the-clock basis of racks to carry torpedoes and racks to carry depth bombs. I think it was significant that history records a miniature Japanese submarine trying to enter Pearl Harbor was sunk by one of our patrol planes carrying a destroyer type depth charge on its wing. He recognized it as a Japanese submarine that was submerged, so he let fly and the submarine was sunk. That was really the first American use of aerial depth charges in World War II to my knowledge.

Q: That was an interesting development and a new dimension to the reconnaissance concept, wasn't it?

Adm. R.: Yes. Well, this is the kind of thing that it was my privilege to participate in, and my interest in guided missiles - missiles of all kinds - was heightened when I was sent to the Bureau of Ordnance for duty. I was the assistant to the Admiral for R & D for all aviation ordnance and also of all ship based guided missiles then being developed by the Bureau of Ordnance.

Q: Was this the Regulus?

Adm. R.: No, the Regulus was a Bureau of Aeronautics missile. The BuOrd missiles were the three T systems, Terrier, Tartar and Talos anti-aircraft ship based missiles, the 5-inch air-to-air rocket, which later became useful for air-to-ground work, the 2.75-inch rocket, and various others - quite a few of these rockets and guided missiles (or their followon versions) are in use in the fleet today. As a matter of fact, in some considerable numbers.

That tour in the Bureau of Ordnance research and development heightened my interest in guided-missile work. It gave me additional visibility to people who were running the Navy, and I presume that these kind of experiences, which were just among a few, brought me to the attention in a favorable way of folks who were in the process of selecting someone to head up what later became known as the Navy's Polaris Program.

Q: In this tour of duty in BuOrd, is this where you acquired an ability to deal with scientists, which is a very special ability?

Adm. R.: Perhaps. We certainly had to form close working relationships with scientists.

Q: This was one of the requisites for the Polaris job, I understand.

Adm. R.: During World War II I was brought back to Washington for a year to establish and set up an aviation gunnery training school because at the outbreak of World War II I was at Kaneohe and I was shocked to note the lack of training for personnel manning the machine guns in patrol planes, for instance.

For example, on the night of 7 December after the devastating attack one of the pilots called me from Pearl Harbor, saying, "They're sending me out tonight on a mission with people in the waist guns who don't even know how to load the guns! Can't you do something about it!" This was a deplorable state of training, so I determined right then and there - that we had to do something about training all of the patrol plane personnel in the Hawaiian area even though they belonged to other commands. So the next day I started a gunnery training school at Kaneohe by going down and getting my ordnancemen together and fished the machine guns out of the burned out hulks of the patrol planes and set them up on a point at Kaneohe. Then we put a plane in the air to tow sleeves and set these machine guns up on stands on the ground and with ordnancemen standing beside these flight people, we started training gun crews. The idea caught on and other commands in the area happily sent their flight personnel over to join in.

Many innovative things were brought in there. We took gun turrets out of torpedo and patrol planes, electrical gun turrets. We set them up on mounts at this gunnery range which was established right there on the edge of Kaneohe. We shot at sleeves. We taught people to use the same equipment that they were going to use in the air. I emphasize we took the waist enclosure and the guns out of patrol planes and sat them up there and made them shoot from the same kind of thing they were going to use when they were in the air, except they were on the ground and were shooting at sleeves, of course. That was the difference.

We did teach people, though, the basic mechanics of taking care of the guns, how to shoot the guns, and the result was we had trained, when I left there to come back to Washington to head up the Navy's aviation training program, more than 3,000 gunners.

It was heart warming to hear expressions of appreciations from former student fighter pilots from Pensacola and patrol plane personnel on one of my visits to the combat forces at Guadacanal. I must say, however, Jimmy Thach did more for fighter gunnery than anyone else. We all admired his pioneering combat techniques.

Q: In what period of time, was this done at Kaneohe?

Adm. R.: I guess it was about thirteen months or something like that. We put them through an accelerated course, but it was all work. And we had lots of enthusiasm for this because we had a war going on and people realized they had to know how to shoot a gun.

Q: That was the new element that was introduced?

Adm. R.: Sure. It was a real stimulation. And, of course as I have mentioned before my interest toward teaching people how to use machine guns was reflected back to three or four years before when I was at Pensacola and one of the many instructors who taught people how to shoot fixed machine guns from fighter planes by aiming the fighter plane, and how to dive bomb and so forth.

The experience at Kaneohe was followed by duty in the aviation training department in Washington and we established many aviation gunnery schools over the country to teach aviation gunners how to shoot guns from fighters and patrol planes. After about a year the Navy sent me back to sea and I was executive officer in the aircraft carrier Hancock. My long living with gunnery found another area to express itself when I found the machine guns in the fighter planes aboard ship were not being cleaned properly when they returned from combat. They were jamming in the air in actual combat! So I got the aviation ordnancemen around and made sure they knew what they were to do and then checked up on them to see that they did it when their planes returned from combat - that those guns were cleaned with soap and hot water, as they were supposed to be, soap and water and properly oiled, and made into apple-pie shape. The bomb racks also were all checked out after every flight.

I imported some of my old aviation ordnancemen buddies from the United States schools who knew their business, got them ordered out to the ship by name and the result was our aviation ordnance and gunnery department was the pride and joy of the ship.

Q: Heretofore it had been somewhat secondary, had it?

Adm. R.: In my opinion it was a sloppy operation. The object of the whole game of being out there was to have those guns shoot well. Now, the second part of this, of course, was the defensive guns of the ship. The Essex-type carrier was armed with four gun mounts of 5-inch guns and had sponsons containing 40 mms., both twins and quads, and then along the catwalks on the flight deck were reams of 20-mm. guns, which the flight-deck crews manned when we were being attacked.

I noted that in the practice gunnery which we had regularly, shooting at sleeves out in the battle zone when we didn't have live targets to shoot at, that they left considerable to be desired. So I took over groups of these, one at a time, for the gunnery officer, set the boys down, and talked to them like a Dutch uncle and reminded them that if they were going to hit a duck they had to shoot in front of them and they had to keep moving the gun as they were shooting. Now, these 20 mms. were equipped with lead computing sights which would compute the lead to hit a plane provided that one of the men on the guns would turn a knob to keep the wings of the airplane properly matched within two moveable pointers. But in the excitement of combat I'm sure this wasn't being done, so I said, "You just go right on and try to keep those wings circumscribed or bounded by these two pointers, but for the man who's actually moving and shooting the gun I want you to lead the target just like he was shooting ducks. If you're going to miss, miss ahead of the plane. You may hit the guy."

Well, the result was with this toning up of the ship's

gunnery personnel they got so good at shooting down the target sleeves that we were not permitted to shoot at sleeves until all the other ships had finished because every time it came by we shot it down with almost the first burst with 5-inch guns or 40 mms. or 20 mms. They said, "Hancock, no shooting from you until we tell you."

Q: Excellence was a handicap!

Adm. R.: No, it wasn't a handicap but it was a source of great pride to our crew and the tow pilots were happy as they didn't have to stream so many sleeves. It took a lot of time to stream sleeves, so they said you will shoot last. They knew the first pass that the guys would make with the long sleeves being towed, why, down would come the sleeve for we'd shoot it off and they'd have to stream another. Of course, this coupled with special attention and training of lookouts made this aircraft carrier, which of course was a bull's eye for attacking planes - (aircraft carriers were the target for attacking planes) the pride and joy of the task force commander as far as its ability to defend itself and to shoot and shoot well. We knocked down many a plane. We had a great big old fat battleship over there with guns coming out of it from bow to stern and it didn't seem to be hitting anything but when attacking planes jumped us we knocked them down and got direct hits on them. That didn't keep us from getting damaged sometimes because a plane did suicide us, but we hit him solidly but of course he was like a bomb exploding right over the ship. There wasn't much you could do about that.

Q: An early attempt at kamikaze, wasn't it?

Adm. R.: We don't know whether it was a kamikaze or not, but we did hit him and knocked him out of the air but he plunged on into the water. There were several other planes that we hit and knocked out of the air and we got away very fortunately. A bomb would fall on one side and the engine on the other side and all of that, just so we were not touched, sometimes we would hope some burning debris on the deck which was quickly put out and pushed over the side.

I guess these kind of associations with naval weaponery at sea and ashore accumulated to a place where I was just one of the many many officers identified with ordnance and gunnery. So in 1955 when it was decided in Washington that the Navy would join in with the Army in an attempt to use at sea the Army ballistic missile to be developed the Navy looked around for a program manager. The Navy had been able to persuade the then Secretary of Defense to join up with the Army in this project. Secretary Wilson - "Engine Charlie" Wilson, I believe he was popularly called to differentiate him from the Charlie Wilson who was head of General Electric, who was fondly called "Washing Machine" Charlie Wilson - (these were all terms of endearment), of course made this decision a very wise one indeed. I learned later that there was quite a group of people who were pulling for one person or another to head up this Navy endeavor with the Army, to see if they could use it aboard surface vessels converted merchant ship first and later perhaps in submarines. I later learned that the Bureau of Aeronautics then headed up by Admiral Jim Russell, had selected me as his candidate for the project manager. The Bureau of Aeronautics wanted to be the lead bureau in this effort. The Bureau of Ordnance also wanted to be the lead bureau. I'm not sure, but I think a classmate of mine who is now deceased, was their candidate. He was an ordnance PG, and eminently qualified. Although I had served in the Bureau of Ordnance for one year I was not an ordnance PG, yet it was only natural that they would turn towards a competent ordnance PG.

Q: At that time it was thought that it should be an effort within the Navy itself under the direction of some bureau?

Adm. R.: Yes, that's right. A person would have to have the support of a bureau in order to do this - there were a myriad of things to be done, all the way from getting and maintaining personnel, the support of personnel and office supplies, contractual support, and you name it. The bureau of course was the kind of an organization that could provide these services. Admiral Sides, I was told later, was in the middle of this selection. I don't know how he voted, but Admiral Russell told me later that he was sorry not to be designated as the lead bureau, but "they kept him quiet by taking his candidate for the job", which fortunately was me. Then they gave the project to the Bureau of Ordnance.

Now, I was summarily jerked out of my job in Norfolk - operations officer for the C in C Atlantic Fleet told me to come to Washington on the run!

Q: You had to leave in 24 hours or something?

Adm. R.: Well, yes, I was told to get up there overnight. So my wife and I loaded our things in two cars and drove up. The job was explained to me and I was told to go to work. Going to work meant going over to an office in the Bureau of Ordnance and I had one officer, Captain Hassler, who is now retired and living in Sunnyvale, California. He was the one person in Bureau Ordnance who met me. So we started out with an office and one officer. He had been one of the prime movers in the Bureau of Ordnance to try to get the project for the bureau.

Admiral Burke made it very clear, along with Secretary of the Navy Thomas, the high importance and absolute top priority within the Navy and on the national scene that this effort was to have, and I was, of course, to work with the Army who had set up a similar organization in Huntsville, Alabama, under Major General Bruce Medaris, to build a large liquid-fuel (main propulsion engine) ballistic missile which was later named Jupiter. This was supposed to be 1,500-mile bird and it was in direct competition with the Air Force's similar efforts to build a land-based, as the Jupiter was, missile called Thor.

Q: Atlas?

Adm. R.: No, it wasn't Atlas. Atlas was a 2,500-mile bird. This was to be a 1,500-mile similar version.

In any event, there was considerable haste on the part of the Army and the Air Force to be the first to develop a 1,500-mile, land-based ballistic missile, and I'm sure that the imposition of the Secretary of Defense on the Army that Jupiter had to be used aboard ships was not too well appreciated by the Army because undoubtedly to try to make it usable aboard ships at sea would be a hindrance to them. There'd be many navy requirements laid on them which would not be necessary at all for land-based missiles, and this would impede their progress and cause them to probably lose the race to the Air Force as to who was going to be the first to provide a 1,500-mile, land-based ballistic missile.

Q: Admiral, why did the Secretary of Defense impose this upon the Army and the Navy, too?

Adm. R.: I think it was due to the persuasiveness of Admiral Burke and Secretary Thomas. As I understand it, they were out to Admiral Burke's quarters one night and they were discussing the matter that the Navy should have ballistic missiles at sea. There had been many people who had thought of this and wanted to do this. As a matter of fact, they did launch - a large German built liquid-fueled missile from an aircraft carrier, at sea. It was very spectacular but obviously not very practical because of the size of the missile and because the ship moved around too much in the seaway.

So Admiral Burke and Secretary Thomas were persuasive and Secretary Wilson said all right, join up with the Army. The Army, I think, in a way, was pleased to have the Navy's support. Obviously, the two services working together were a formidable group.

Q: Was the Navy equally as pleased to have it a joint project, or would they have preferred to have gone their own way?

Adm. R.: Well, in my opinion the Navy actually didn't know - and had considerable reservations. When you say "the Navy" that takes in a lot of people, but let's say most of the senior officers in Washington, with the exception of Admiral Burke, were not deliriously happy to embark on such a risky and costly venture as this. They felt - and I think very properly so - that a large liquid-fueled missile aboard ship was a very dangerous thing. There were dangers of leaking fuel from pipes and pumping and all this sort of thing, even on the open launching stations, on the deck where this large thin-shelled bird would be erected and held in place and then fueled just before its launch. Conceivably, you'd be in more danger from that than you would if you were under fire from the enemy, and those of us in the Navy project office had reservations too. But national urgency caused us to give it a real try.

As a matter of fact, later on, during our initial tests of mock-ups of the bird and ships' structures we proved very conclusively that in those days the carrying and launching of large liquid-fueled missiles aboard a surface vessel was very, very hazardous because when we'd topple them over to see what would happen and the resulting fire and explosion just made it a very difficult thing to countenance, or to really go ahead with. The thought of putting these missiles in the confined spaces of a submarine underneath the water, would make an internal combustion engine out of the whole submarine. Of course storageable liquid fuels have advanced tremendously since then but the inherent safety of solid fuels still gets my vote.

So, as these tests with liquid fuel engines moved on, we were experimenting with large solid rocket boosters that could become, perhaps, motors for ballistic missiles. Of course, the Terrier, Tartar, and the 2.75, and the 5-inch HVAR rockets were all solid-propelled boosters, so the Navy was not entirely ignorant of the capabilities of solid propellants. But the specific impulse or "oomph" of the motors built for solid propellants was not nearly as high as the isp that you could get from liquid fuels. However, solid fuel motors were far more safe and we had had some considerable experience in handling them aboard ship and aboard airplanes, so that the Office of Naval Research, in some of their work, with Atlantic Research

Corporation, which is in the vicinity of Washington, fortunately about a year after we had been working on liquid fuel motors came up with some rather startling advances in the specific impulse that you could get from solid propellants.

The rule was formerly that the addition of a substance like powder aluminum in solid propellants, up to a certain point you could get an increase in specific impulse. The people down there said, well, what would happen if you put massive amounts of aluminum powder in it? So they did that -

Q: Ignoring that cut-off point and going ahead beyond it?

Adm. R.: Yes - They ignored what the textbook said, so they went ahead and came up with a marked improvement in the amount of specific impulse, which clearly showed to us that now it was possible to build large solid fuel motors that could propel a large missile some 1,200 to 1,500 nautical miles.

Q: This, incidentally, was achieved by two young scientists, was it not, Rumbeau and Henderson?

Adm. R.: I think so, yes, under the sponsorship of the Office of Naval Research.

We delightedly seized upon this and went to work with our principals in the contractual family which we had by this time gathered around us to try to put the Jupiter to sea and to our delight, we came up with a very, very much smaller missile carrying a respectable warhead and one which would be entirely safe to put into submarines. It was very obvious to us that putting ballistic missiles in surface vessels was not nearly as attractive as putting them in submarines, because, one, the submarine was more difficult to find, and, secondly, if we could launch it submerged - while the submarine was submerged - the missile would have a very stable platform because at very few feet below the water the submarine is a very stable platform. It's not rolling around storm-tossed as the surface vessel would be.

So we directed our attention to this matter and evolved a program putting solid-propellant ballistic missiles into submarines. I very proudly carried this over to Admiral Burke and the Secretary of the Navy, and then to Secretary of Defense Wilson. I contrasted it with the previous program which he had approved for us to go ahead and showed him a series of slides of what it would do for size and costs of the vessels and where we could use it and how, and we could use it in submarines. The last slide showed the contrast with the program he had approved, that we could put it into submarines and we could save upwards to $50,000,000.

Q: Was it not 500,000,000?

Adm. R.: No, it was 50,000,000 for the liquid fuel missile placed in surface ships.

In any event when I finished the presentation, the Secretary of Defense looked most appreciative and he said, "Well, Admiral, you've shown me a lot of sexy slides this morning, but I tell you that last slide where you showed that tremendous saving, was the sexiest one of all."

Q: Money speaks!

Adm. R.: We walked out feeling very good indeed about this and, in due time, he indicated that he would give his approval to the dissolution of our working partnership with the Army and to proceed on our own. Acceptance of this program in the Navy, however, was coming along not as well as we had hoped. Admiral Burke called a meeting of all of his senior flag officers in his office and had me there, I guess as the piece de resistance, and he told them what we planned to do and sought their advice. Of course, this was typical of Admiral Burke. He didn't try to "bull" his way through. He tried to get people to see things as he saw them and tried to explain the rationale behind this thinking, hoping that they would come to the same conclusion that he did.

He asked them at the end of his dissertation on what we planned to do and sought their advice what they would advise him to do. Not one of them was enthusiastic about this program.

Q: Why?

Adm. R.: Most of them felt that it would be a waste of money, a tremendous drain on the Navy's budget, and that it would not be successful. The result would be that many things that they needed in their areas of responsibility would not be purchased or would not be done, and the Navy would get a big black eye out of this program, and they so expressed themselves to Admiral Burke.

Q: The overriding issue of national defense didn't - ?

Adm. R.: It wasn't that so much. They too were participating in national defense. They had charge of building submarines and destroyers and aircraft and aircraft carriers, and so on, and to take literally millions and millions of dollars and put it in something they were not convinced would be successful - it was a normal reaction. After all, launching a missile from a submarine while it was submerged was an entirely new idea. It had never been done, and so on. There were so many things that had yet to be proven.

Q: At the time of this conference, had the Secretary of Defense ordered the funds for the development of this missile to come from the Navy budget?

Adm. R.: Well, of course, it was obvious to everybody that the initial funds would have to come from the existing Navy budget to get started until the new fiscal year came around. I'm sure that this played a major part in the attitudes of the admirals because they could see so many of their cherished programs going down the drain, which were quite important and no one can say that they weren't. It was not selfishness. They had a responsibility for a certain part of the Navy and it was obvious that it was important and proper that they speak up for their part of the Navy.

Q: Were you invited to speak your piece at that conference?

Adm. R.: At the end of it, as a sort of finale, Admiral Burke turned to me and said, what do you think. And, in my youthful enthusiasm, I said that "if the Navy didn't go ahead with it it would be making the biggest mistake it had ever made." With that we were dismissed, and Burke then decreed that we would proceed and proceed with top priority, and wrote a memorandum to that effect. He sent me a copy and it dictated, in effect, that I was to have absolute top priority on anything I wanted to do and everyone in the Navy would be responsive to my requests. If they found that they could not be, they were to come instantly to him with me and he would take it on himself to say no if he thought it was proper.

Obviously, this was a "magic" piece of paper. I carried it in my shirt pocket for days and weeks and months. I only had to show it once or twice and sort of apologetically, you know, the boss has told me to do this. And "gosh, this is something I've just got to do and I hope you understand." Of course, we were given carte blanche on everything, including people that we wanted to come in. We asked that people be ordered in from all over the United States. I got one gent off of a destroyer off the south coast of Africa. He was flown back and put to work.

Q: How did the admirals who had opposed the idea react to this?

Adm. R.: Well, actually, they were a fine group of people, as admirals, as a rule, are. Once the boss had made up his mind they fell in behind him on this program quite well. This didn't stop all the bickering, this didn't make me immediately a "hero". Everybody thought well of it, of course. They had their reservations, but they had their orders, so they carried out their orders, and I think this is to their great credit.

The thing, I think, that shook them up most of all was that no one had anything to say about the program except me. No one in the Navy could tell me "what" or "how" to do this.

Q: This was completely innovative as far as the Navy went.

Adm. R.: Completely. We had complete, absolute authority, and no one was to look over our shoulders and try to tell us how to do something or what to do.

Q: I take it there was no precedent for this at all?

Adm. R.: No, no precedent before and, I think, after.

Q: In any one of the services?

Adm. R.: I would think that's right. There were several similar examples along about that time, but they didn't have the complete authority that was given to me, I know for sure. General Schriever had something similar to that, but he had to come and plead and beg whoever was head of the air staff, I know, on many occasions. He had something quite similar and perhaps to him, working within the Air Force command, it was similar and was equivalent. I don't know. But, to me, this was absolute authority. I had the authority of the Secretary of Defense, as authority is currently now known, and this innovation and responsibility, I think was one of the keynotes - key factors - of getting this program off to a fast start and its performance of the military-industrial team, which has continued to this day.

Q: Obviously, the results proved that point. I wonder, for the sake of this story, Sir, if you wouldn't want to lap back at this time and deal with your first concern, which was the joint effort with the Army and Jupiter - going back to December of 1955 and so forth, because this development that you've just described was the end of 1956.

Adm. R.: Yes. Well, we worked with the Army for the best part of a year. We set up a cadre of officers down at Huntsville and I made many trips down there myself to be sure that we were working together in the best possible way and to ensure that our requirements levied on the missile's characteristics were properly understood and were being met by the Army so that we might have the best chance of using this missile.

Q: What was your own attitude on this? Were you optimistic that it could be accomplished, for the Jupiter?

Adm. R.: My attitude was let's give it a fair trial. This was the direction in which we were pointed by both the Navy and the Army, and so it was our responsibility to develop the idea to the maximum extent to be sure that it would go, that it would work or would not work. And this we did. The Army gave us, I thought, very fine cooperation, although we were a hindrance to them obviously. We had to do a lot of extra work and a lot of extra study. Dr. von Braun was then the chief technical officer to General Medaris, and considering the circumstances the relationship between the Army and the Navy was very good. Obviously it was not a happy one for them exactly because we did slow them down and they were in a race with the Air Force. And it was not happy for us because we were trying to take somebody else's missile which was specifically being designed primarily for use from land against land targets and we were trying to pump some salt water into it so that we could take it to sea! That was a tough job and -

Q: Can you cite anything specific in the way of these problems?

Adm. R.: No. They were mainly personal problems - problems

of education. We would say we need this characteristic and the Army engineers and people would say, well, why, why in the world do you need it, you're going to cause us to go back and re-do all of this, that, and the other. So it was an educational process which was, at times, a little painful, particularly when the folks were in a hurry and obviously our requirements were slowing them down - and expensive, too.

It was a natural thing but, as I said before, under the circumstances I think our relationships worked out very well indeed. As a matter of fact, most of those people are good personal friends of mine right today. But I'm sure they had a sigh of relief when it was determined we were going to go our own way because then they were unfettered and released. They could proceed to optimize the weapon for their own use without any further hindering requirements for naval use.

Q: When you were working with the Army on this joint project, how did you and your fellow officers and scientists develop the overriding wisdom of the Navy's end of it? Tell me about that.

Adm. R.: We established a contractual family, an industry contractual family, to develop the application of the Jupiter missile. It was not a full contractual family such as we had in Polaris because the Army had already selected the missile contractor, which was Chrysler. They had selected the guidance contractor, and they had the engines contractor, which was North American Aviation (at that time). So we had nothing to say about the selection of the industrial partners.

Q: You had to work along with them!

Adm. R.: We had to work along with them, and one of the things we did to make sure of an optimum relationship was to ask Chrysler if they would also be our (the Navy) missile contractor - prime contractor, because inasmuch as they were building the thing for the Army we didn't want to have one group going and explaining what we wanted to another group. We explained it to the same group and the same group of engineers and were then trying to work out both problems.

Q: Did this not result in some confusion in their minds, in industry? I mean they were riding two horses, were they not?

Adm. R.: No, not so much confusion. It would have been more confusing had we had another company than Chrysler. They were working for the same boss and they were being motivated by the same boss, I mean their own bosses, civilian bosses, and they were being told by their civilian bosses to please both customers. So they had a motivation - I'm talking about the Chrysler people - they had a motivation for both customers. The result was you got more cooperation at the working level than you would if you had another contractor, civilian contractor, come in and try to tell them what their client wanted them to do. The principal contractor would resent that.

Q: I see. It would have been kind of chaotic if you'd had another contractor.

Adm. R.: It would have been terrible if we'd got another prime contractor other than Chrysler. That was just sort of a "warm-up" phase - it actually turned out to be a "warm-up" phase. We learned a lot, and when it came time to go into the Polaris effort, the bird which we later named Polaris -

Q: Which you named, I understand?

Adm. R.: Yes - we started with using some of the solid propellant motors, having got approval for the program by the Secretary of Defense and the Secretary of the Navy and the Chief of Naval Operations, we then took about three weeks to select our own industrial family, our associates. We not only had to have a missile contractor, we had to have a warhead contractor, we had to have a missile-guidance contractor, and a missile-launching contractor. We were going to do something that had never been done before, and that was to launch large ballistic missiles from a submarine when it was submerged. We had to have a navigational contractor because the submarine was supposed to stay submerged for long periods of time, and we had to know with great precision where it was at all times and have the ability to update the navigational position with minimum exposure of the submarine at regular intervals and this depended on how good the navigational equipment aboard ship was - of course we had to select that contractor.

The selection of various contractors for this widely diversified program involving a missile that had never been built, a navigational system which would precisely locate the position of the submarine, a fire control system to resolve the information to inform the missile what it should do to land on target, and a missile guidance system which would take this information and steer the missile until it told the solid propellant motors to cut themselves off with precise timing in order that the warhead would follow a ballistic course to the target -- all involved pushing back the frontiers of science to a degree and scope which had never before been done.

To select the contractual family of industry working in partnership with the Navy, had to be done with great care but at the same time, because of the urgency of the program, it had to be done on an expedited basis. There was no time for a long drawnout formal competition between various companies for these several elements of the overall weapons systems. And indeed it would have taken literally years to have come up with anything remotely resembling what we actually did develop because of the lack of experience in science and technology at that time. So happily we used the common sense method of selection of contractors which involved an intense scrutiny of the capabilities of various companies, and importantly, the work-load which they already had in-house which would be in competition for their top technical people with our program.

Fortunately our small group of naval officers and civil service engineers were quite well-informed on the various companies who showed an interest in our program and they constituted a review board which gave each of the civilian contractor companies a day to come in and tell us of their ideas of how these unknown developments could best be tackled. Importantly, they also were required to give us a list of names of top technical people who would be dedicated to this job.

So in a period of about one month we were able to sort out with considerable accuracy those who were best fitted to take major prime contractual roles in the various major elements of this entire weapons system, i.e., the missile in its entirety with sub-primes for the solid propellant motors and the guidance package, the navigational system contractor, the fire control and missile guidance contractor, the launching and handling contractor who would develop a successful means of shooting a missile from a submerged submarine and, importantly, a program office management concept to manage this entire program through the major subsystem prime contractors.

When a program as innovative as this is initiated it really doesn't make much sense, if time is of importance, to conduct long drawn-out competition between many contractors and then have a couple of C-130 aircraft fly them to Washington where they will be studied for another year or so before the contractual family is selected. I consider this a very wasteful way of doing business because the technical approaches finally selected will largely be obsolescent by this time and as the program goes on, a major part of this work will have to be discarded with millions of dollars of our taxpayers money wasted and the program in effect set back timewise because of this unnecessary and over-cautious approach.

So with our contractual family selected in my program office, my first impulse was to go over and tell the Secretary of the Navy who we had chosen, but then it occurred to me that he had given me all of his authority in writing to act for him on all matters pertaining to this project. So I said why in the heck should I abrogate part of this responsibility, so we wrote a telegram and put our selected contractors under contract, over my signature, and sent them out!

Then, I went over and told the Secretary of the Navy, and, as usual, he had me ushered in promptly. No matter what he was doing he always excused the people who were there and said, "Show Admiral Raborn in. He has top priority." It was a little embarrassing at times to have senior admirals shooed out of his office and walk in. I was a "frocked" admiral then. (I'd been selected for admiral. I was wearing an admiral's uniform, but because I had not yet made my number, I was drawing a captain's pay!). I went in and told the Secretary of the Navy that we'd made the selections for the team and that we had put them under contract.

He looked at me with a startled and surprised look and said, "I thought I had some responsibility for that." I said, "Yes, Mr. Secretary, you certainly have but, you recall, you delegated your complete authority and responsibility to me and I have exercised it. Here are the people who are now under contract to us." He looked over the list, looked up and beamed and said, "Well, you sure made some good choices, no question about it. I recognize those people. They're all good people."

That was the way this thing was done. What a contrast to todays drawn out, expensive to the taxpayers, "Follow the book" way of doing business!

Q: Did you include on that list any of the contractors who were working for Jupiter, too? Was Chrysler on your list?

Adm. R.: No, Chrysler was not. We chose Lockheed for the missile contractor and chose Westinghouse for the submerged launching contractor. Also I had gone up to talk to Dr. Stark Draper at MIT Instrumentation Laboratory about taking on the technical job of evolving the missile guidance. He had done some very fine work, to my knowledge, on inertial platforms, inertial guidance work, and he agreed to take on the missile guidance job. We brought in the General Electric Company, the Pittsfield GE division, to be his industrial back-up, to actually manufacture the gyros and accelerometers in production that were to go into the missiles - and the inertial tables to go into the missile guidance package, but all of this was to be under his technical direction, because he was and still is the world's leading technical genius on inertial platforms for missile guidance. (It is interesting to note that this Polaris guidance team were later hired by N.A.S.A. to guide the astronauts to the moon and back!)

We selected Aerojet General for the missile propulsion, to build the solid fuel propellant motors. We had instrumentation people, Interstate Electronics, who were to do the instrumentation of our ranger and ships and so forth, and they're still doing that job for the Poseidon.

This whole contractural family was kept together and we obtained from them promises of a completely dedicated group of people and separate buildings for our work. We constructed the buildings as necessary to put them into business in order that our work could be absolutely segregated from the rest of the contractor's work and be given absolute top priority in their plants. We established on-site naval-civilian representatives of our own, naval officers in small teams, to follow their work on a day-to-day basis and, of course, we had a small team here in Washington. We had truly a magnificent military-industrial partnership.

Q: Were there any repercussions to your selectees once they became known? Some of the concerns that had worked and were working for the Army, did they not feel they should be in on this particular project?

Adm. R.: No, we had no reverberations whatsoever.

Q: None from the congressional area?

Adm. R.: No, none whatsoever. I think that there's entirely

too much made about this today. I think that the idea of competition for competition's sake is time-consuming, expensive, and sometimes, particularly if you put the award of contracts on the lowest price without due regard for capability, you are buying a very bad thing for the defense posture and the taxpayer. As a matter of fact, it's one of the most uneconomical things and wasteful things you can do - to take somebody who really doesn't know what the problems are all about and, due to ignorance, they in effect "buy" in, and you are required by law to give it to the lowest bidder. This is the most wasteful thing that you can do. No one who's building a house, if he advertised for bids, would take a guy who obviously had no record of success to speak of. Just to take his bid because he the lowest would be the most foolish thing you could do and he'd know it. Well, if you can translate that to a major program dealing in new and unknown technology, you can see how silly it is to slavishly follow "standard procedures" instead of exercising judgement! It is impossible to cast out a R & D program. We've been building houses for 3,000 years or more, but we still have boo-boos and over-runs in houses. For example, if you want to get a surgical operation done on your body, you don't go to the cheapest surgeon, you go to the best surgeon that you can interest in your case. National defense deserves equally first class care. Otherwise the corporate body could become corpus delicti!

So the selection of the Polaris team was that kind of a thing. We got the best we could for the country, to our judgment, and they in turn have distinctly proven to this country and to anyone who wants to look into it on an unbiased basis that this kind of awarding of contracts is the best way to go, because I believe the Polaris contractural team have performance unequaled by any contractual family of a major project before or since. In their performance-time schedules they consistently underran those set for the program. And this performance was obtained by cultivating a real team spirit and effort! Today people want to set up all kinds of managerial techniques which are theoretical in nature and by men who frequently have had little or no practical experience in managing programs. These elaborate and theoretical procedures enforced upon program managers hinder rather than help get the job done. Of course they are supposed to prevent a manager from making mistakes, and this is ridiculous. It seems to assume that everyone is inexperienced, so you have to go through a set routine in order to get anything done. This kind of slavish devotion to check off lists permits no exercise of brains and literally costs us taxpayers millions of dollars. It penalizes the armed forces of the United States for they are not as fully armed and fully equipped as they could be if people could use good judgment instead of endless reviews by others. Much money is being wasted by unnecessary competitive efforts and wasteful allocation of contracts to incompetent "low bidder" people. That's what's going on right now under the guise of, "well, this is the way the 'book' says to do it." The best way by whose standards? Performance? Certainly not! The various echelons of review seem to feel that only they are competent to pass on the program actions.

The lessons of Polaris have certainly been lost on this country. It was a very successful effort of major proportions - But now people seem to be more content to "stooge" along following the many rules, feeling "protected" while more bureaucrats write more rules to prevent mistakes as if there can ever be a substitute for common sense.

Q: Has it been because it hasn't been publicized to that extent, or what?

Adm. R.: People don't want to work this way. There are millions of people in the government - and while I say "millions," I guess it's at least a million people in the government - whose jobs are built up on this bureaucracy of paper work and endless reviews of the program managers work. Their jobs would be jeopardized if they streamlined action taking and did things in a more common sense, straight-forward way. So, obviously we are not going to get this kind of thing turned around. We have unbelievable management "top-hamper" in the Government. They don't want to believe any other way can be successful or profitable, except the way that they are sponsoring. So we have procedural papers and procedural reviews and methodology which is the most wasteful thing that I know of in this country, absolutely the most wasteful, under the guise of efficiency! It's the most inefficient thing that I know of, and no one can get anything done, from building a house to developing a new major weapon system under these kind of procedures and do it efficiently and do it effectively, and do it effectively against time. Talk about inefficiency in defense procurement. How does the civilian metro system in Washington, D. C. compare? Or take a look at the new senate office building job over-runs.

In the Polaris program we knocked some three and a half years off the program schedule, and this was not a stereotyped program such as building subways! This was an innovative, completely new, never been done before weapon system. We didn't know how to navigate submarines with precision while submerged, we didn't know how to launch a large missile submerged in the water, we didn't know how to guide it once it got into the air and deliver it with adequate accuracy, we didn't have a warhead for it - a nuclear warhead. None of these things had been done before and yet naval officers in uniform, civil service managed their contractors and it was done superbly well by this consortium of military and industrial family. And we had "letter" contracts for about the first two years. As a matter of fact many of our management techniques are now "standard procedures" in civilian industry. We simply brought out the latent talent in people and gave them performance goals to reach without crippling and excessive supervision. Many people have asked wasn't this expensive? and I said, "Sure, it was expensive, but we were spending at the rate of 1.2 billion dollars a year and we produced the system three and a half years ahead the original schedule, so we saved six and a half or seven billion dollars, just in time alone." So, how much money did we waste? I don't think we wasted much. I think we saved a hell of a lot of money. The Country had a weapon system which it needed, when it needed it! How much is our countrys safety worth!

Importantly, we got this system in the hands of the Navy and the country for its defense in a very timely way. It is vital to recognize that it is not important what you've got on the drawing board or in test, when "the balloon goes up" - as we used to say in World War II, when the balloon goes up - you only can fight with what you have in adequate quantity in the hands of the troops. And yet now we have people in high places who are so entranced with all of these procedural matters of management, procedural matters of competition, and mountains and mountains of paper work now required in weapon proposals. As if these are the important things. The cart is before the horse! The efforts of all those procurement people could be better spent toward doing the thing that has to be done, and you save two to three years on every major program and literally millions of dollars. More importantly the military services would have much needed weapons in hand to defend our Democracy!

Q: What was the overriding consideration which caused you to set aside the established way of doing things and go about your work directly?

Adm. R.: Well, we were told that this was of the utmost urgency for the defense of our country that we bring this weapon system into existence at the earliest possible time. So we didn't spend time about working on procedures. We spent time on working on the job to be done. We said, "well" - and we were all men of some experience - "what's the best way to do it?" "All right, let's do it that way." The staff which we had assembled around ourselves was small but highly talented, they didn't have to go and hold formal one to two year competitions to know what was the best thing to do. They had enough experience to say, all right, let's select these contractors and proceed along these lines and learn more about it as technical "savvy" is applied to the job. We went slowly at first but more rapidly as things fit into place. It can be compared to flying an airplane from one place to another. The plane can climb to altitude over the airfield before proceeding, or it can climb enroute to the altitude needed.

Q: Admiral, what did you learn in the way of techniques during this initial year when you were working with the Army? Was there anything of particular importance that you could apply when you got working on Polaris?

Adm. R.: Oh, I think any effort engaged in over a period of a year, as that was, you're bound to learn some things. It would be, I think, silly to say that a man can live a whole year and not learn anything. We were exposed to the Army's way of controlling their programmes, managing their programmes, and I'm sure this was helpful. We were exposed to industry, firms that were interested and talented in this kind of work and this was helpful. We operated in this environment, the military-industrial environment, of big missiles which gave us a lot of insight into the capabilities of firms. It added to our store of knowledge and I think it was a very good warm-up, although we didn't use any of those contractors for Polaris because none of them were particularly fitted, we thought, for the specialized application of a submarine launched solid propellant missile that we were going to use.

Q: You speak of "we" constantly, perhaps this would be a time, then, to talk about the team that you began to assemble around you in this initial year.

Adm. R.: Here, again, we were given this job of top priority in the Navy and co-equal to any in the country. We looked around and said, who do we want to assist us? I needed a good deputy, and Captain J. B. Colwell came to my attention. (Later vice admiral). I had known of him and favorably. He was a man of mature, calm judgment, a wise man. So I asked that he be ordered in. Obviously, the admiral for whom he was working was not too happy about this and I heard about that in no uncertain terms. I had been told that his then Admiral boss would be approached by another admiral and told about this before the orders were issued, but unfortunately that didn't occur.

So Captain Colwell came in, and then we started selecting

our technical in-house team, a technical director and assistant and we chose then (Captain Grayson Merrill and Levering Smith) by the same kind of familiarity with their past accomplishments. We looked for a good top civilian (civil service), one who knew money management, who knew comptroller duties and planning duties, and the name of Gordon Pehrson came to mind. He was then working for the Army over in the Chief of Staff's office to assist them in their planning. I read some of the work that he was doing for the Army and realized that he was a very astute planner.

Q: You didn't know him personally?

Adm. R.: I didn't know him personally. So I asked him would he come over and let me talk to him. This he did and we told him what we wanted, that we wanted a "top" civilian. He would run the administrative planning side of the house. He would be the comptroller, he would be the planner, have the management of funds, of budgets, contracts, the whole thing, and he would be the counterpart of the technical director and support the technical director in doing his job.

He was persuaded to come over and I promised him a GS-17 classification if he could come and I had the devil of a time getting that billet and other civil service billets approved. I had to go through the White House to get the Civil Service Commission to give me a GS-17 billet. They, the lower level civil service people, just rebelled, they wouldn't do it. A "super grade civilian" was just out of the question to them. So I had a friend in the White House and he, in turn, got hold of the chairman of the Civil Service Commission and said to him, in effect, your organization is holding up the Polaris program. You ought to go down to see what they are trying to do and you ought to help. So he sent his Number Two man over. I explained to him why we needed the civil service billets and what jobs we wanted them to have, why we wanted men of this quality, and the GS-17 billet, too. He called in the local Civil Service people who passed on these things and "dressed them" down in my presence and said, you go out and prepare the paper work for every one of the Civil Service billets that Admiral Raborn has requested and have them ready pronto. You're not to go home or leave your offices until they are ready and over in my hands. This kind of action was unheard of. In other words, the billets, descriptions, and the justification for them, which we had previously given the Civil Service people had not been moving with any speed. But now they were required to stay there until they were finished! So we got a GS-17 and we got every one of our civilian billets approved overnight.

It took that kind of action. I didn't know the Chairman of the Civil Service system, but Americans can move when necessary. The Civil Service Commission proved it to us all. Need I say more?

Q: Do you want to name him, the White House contact. He was

a great help.

Adm. R.: Yes, he was a great help. He's now deceased. We needed friends, so I went out of my way to introduce people such as him to the program, with what we were then envisioning to accomplish and how important it was to our country.

Q: Did you have to use White House influence any other time?

Adm. R.: No, we did not. It was not necessary, as a matter of fact. Importantly though, the secretary of the National Security Council did interest himself in our work and I took the pains to go over to his office and keep him and the members of his staff up to date on how we were doing. This I continued to do that when Dr. Gordon Gray was the secretary of the Security Council for President Eisenhower.

It was apparent to me that it was most necessary that important people in government - science and industry, who could speak a good word for you and help you - had to be acquainted with this program and its status. I took a major role in this. I had a little "road show", which I kept updating, of about thirty minutes and did it all myself bringing along only my good buddy, the civilian who ran the viewgraph machine and slide projector, etc.

Q: And you lectured?

Adm. R.: Yes - Anybody who seemed to be reluctant about the

program or had reason to be kept up-dated. I took it on myself to seek an audience with him and explain what we were doing - how we were doing it and why we were doing it. This took me even to the Secretary of the Treasury, the National Security Council, members of Congress, particularly all the members of the Congress that had a direct responsibility in our program.

Q: Did you appear before committees?

Adm. R.: Well, yes. But what I was describing was informal and in addition to formal committee appearances. I always tried to brief the chairmen and their staffs before formal appearances, so that they might have a better idea of what they were going to hear and they would know the status of the program and thus hopefully make the formal hearings go more smoothly, and this indeed it did. They could prepare their questions, etc. I briefed Carl Vinson and his staff, chairman George Mahan and his staff, Senator and Chairman Stennis and his staff, and others. They all became intensely interested in the program, and a major reason why this program went so smoothly was that everyone connected with or had anything to do at all with the program, from the executive branch of the government to the congressional branch and into the military industrial contractual family, were all informed of the true status of the program. Complete honesty within one organization and to those above us was our watch word! We were convinced that if everyone connected with the program were properly informed it would go better.

So we had a very planned, methodical campaign which was carried on by a whole cadre of officers who always made themselves available to go and talk on Polaris. I took it on myself to keep the people in Washington officialdom constantly up to date on our problems and how we were solving them and our successes (or failures), this included the Bureau of the Budget.

In this way, the people who were actually working in the program made it a part of their lives. It was their program. They became involved in it. In our industrial family, as well as our military, we had dedication talks. For instance, we would send out a top man from Washington (and I myself would go sometimes), and we'd have the entire Polaris work in a factory on a Saturday morning close down. We'd have all the management and workmen. They were asked to invite their families, wives and children to be present for the presentation. Sometimes there were loud-speaker systems or closed-circuit television systems set up - or whatever system was proper and available. Then we would explain the whole concept of the program. I or someone from my office would explain - the "big" picture and tell them what was being done to bring this weapon system into being and why it was so necessary for our country, for them.

Then the local manager would get up and tell them about their company's part in this over-all big program, with the emphasis on how necessary it was for their (the people's) future, the preservation of this country, importance to the future of this country, the continuance of our way of life, etc. This was a major weapon system designed to play a major role in protecting our country and to protect them individually.

In this way, we involved the families of the people who were working on Polaris, both military and civilian folks.

Q: Psychologically, that was wonderful!

Adm. R.: Yes - in these meetings we would have soft drinks and cookies for the kids. After the talks, papa would take mama and the kids and show them where he worked, at what lathe, or where or what he did. This Polaris program then became well known. We required dedicated performance on the part of all of our people, our officers and civil service everywhere, our home office people and importantly the industrial family. So when a wife would note a neighbor would come home at 4:30 every afternoon and her husband working on the Polaris program would get home at six or seven o'clock -- or maybe they wouldn't get home that night! She naturally needed motivating too! We worked Saturdays, all day, and sometimes we worked on Sundays. This took its toll until we hit upon this idea of motivation, and the result of the motivation was that the families were proud that their husband was working on this program. Many a time, I'm told, when a guy maybe had one too many to drink the night before, he'd ask his wife to call in and tell them he was sick, and she'd say, "Get out of bed and go to work. You've got an important job to do for us." So, he'd be sent in to work!

This motivation thing was a very real effort on our part and it paid off in dividends far beyond anything that I can begin to express in these few words. If I'd find an officer some place and it seemed to me that he was not "up to speed" and not doing the job, I'd call him into my office, sit him down, and I'd go over the whole thing with him. "Evangelistic" fervor, that's the way we approached it. I got him wound up real good and sent him out and let him go do his job. They became like tigers. As a matter of fact I called them "my tigers."

Q: This use of motivation like that, how did you arrive at it? Did it spring from your roots in the Bible Belt?

Adm. R.: I guess. A lot of my family are evangelistic preachers, Baptists preachers, gospel singers. We all love fried chicken!

So we became "tigers" and the "tiger" became a symbol. Everybody everywhere had a little toy tiger on their desk, a little tiger symbol. We went after our work like "tigers."

Q: Talking about briefing people and giving them a picture of what you were doing, did you get to the President -- was General Eisenhower interested?

Adm. R.: Yes. General Eisenhower was quite interested in this work because he initiated it and he called us in and had General Schriever, General Medaris, and I, in one day at a Security Council meeting and asked us to make a presentation of our programs, which we did in the White House, in the Cabinet room. I remember how struck I was at the evident youth of General Schriever. He's young looking for his age, very young looking for his age, and I'd never met him before. When he came outside and we'd left the presence of the President, I turned to General Schriever in mock seriousness and said, "You daggone Air Force generals give me a pain." He looked at me and kind of wondered "what in the world's wrong with him!" I said, "You and your youthful appearances make us old admirals look as old as we actually are!"

That was the first time we'd ever met, so we became good friends and have remained so ever since!

Q: You spoke before about going to the Secretary of the Treasury - and that was George Humphrey -

Adm. R.: Well, at that time, it was the former deputy Secretary of Defense, the Texan, who was Secretary of the Treasury. Bob Anderson.

Q: Why did you select him?

Adm. R.: It was timely. The program was growing by leaps and bounds and the need for money was getting to be quite sizable, and I just thought, well, it wouldn't be a bad thing because of his former tour as deputy secretary of defense and he was in the high councils, to have him speak a good word for us would be fine. So I called him up and said, "Would you like to see what we're doing, what program we're planning for next year? You've got to print the money." He said, "Send it over." So I sent over the program for the upcoming year. Then I had second thoughts on it because I hadn't yet exposed it to the Secretary of Defense! So I told one of my friends in the Secretary of the Defense's office, "Would you mention to him that the Secretary of the Treasury indicated he'd like to see it and I thought it would be the courteous and gracious thing to do." He promised he would, but it turned out two or three weeks later when the Secretary of Defense and I were going to inspect the Lockheed installation on the West Coast, that I found out from my friend who accompanied him that he had not told the Secretary of my informing the Secretary of Treasury. So riding in the car from San Francisco to Sunnyvale, I mentioned this subject to the Secretary of Defense, the Honorable Neil McElroy. He became rather disturbed about this. I won't say he was angry. He certainly contained himself. And I said, "Well, I recognized that maybe you had better things to do and hadn't had a chance to review it. So I will retrieve the document immediately. Obviously I didn't want him to get it from the Secretary of the Treasury that he had seen the program before SecDef had looked at it. This was a mistake on my part and my enthusiasm for keeping people informed got out of step this time. A good lesson for me!

It behooves anyone trying to do a job of this kind to ensure that people who are going to pass on it are kept well informed on program status and plans! This includes the then

Bureau of the Budget - I used to go and talk to Mr. George in the Bureau of the Budget who was assigned the job of reviewing Polaris. I used to go and talk over our budget and explain to him what we were going to do and why, and this was the bill for the work contemplated. Well, we got fine cooperation from the Bureau of the Budget. We got no nit-picking whatsoever, one, because Mr. George is a man of great stature, and he made this become one of his programs for personal review.

Q: You have some political instincts, too, I believe!

Adm. R.: Perhaps. Maybe this story will illustrate.

I well remember a trip to Hughes Aircraft Company. At long last, they got a job - we decided we'd have a back-up in the submarine fire control and missile guidance work. I'd like to emphasize that we had lots of competition in industry. We generated our own competition in industry after we got started. For instance, the guidance platform was a very difficult thing to do. As a matter of fact, the gyros and accelerometers that went on the platform were very, very difficult to manufacture, and we had five major companies trying to build them and there were only about two that wound up being able to do it.

We wanted to have an alternate supplier for the guidance package, which includes the inertial table and the electronics. So we chose to team Honeywell and Hughes Aircraft. Honeywell was to build the stable table, and Hughes to build electronics. Well, in due time, as was my custom, I made regular tours of the industry team who were making the parts and so I went by Hughes and our old friend L. A. "Pat" Hyland - he's still out there and running a good show - said, "Would you like to see your work?" I said, "Sure."

So we went down and there on this very large floor was a block of about 300 girls working, and they were in assembly lines making the electronics that were going on this small inertial table in the missile guidance. I noticed as I walked through the line, being escorted by the supervisor, who was a woman, that all the girls at the work benches were dressed in red, white, and blue middy blouses and skirts. I remarked on this and said, "Why is this that they're all in this patriotic uniform?" And she said, "We're so proud to be a part of the Polaris family that we decided on our own that we'd go buy these and we wear them every Wednesday."

I said, "Gee, but this is Thursday." She said, "Well, we heard you were coming." "So we wore them to show you how proud we are to be a part of the Polaris program!"

They had a picture taken of them, all of them in a large group, and they all signed their name on the back of it with a little dedication message, dedicating their best efforts to this wonderful program. I think that's symbolic of the kind of motivation we had of the people on the factory floor. They would knock themselves out to do a good job, and they did. It's people who do the job. People turn out their best efforts if they're properly motivated and managed. Then you've an unbeatable team.

That was just absolutely symbolic of the whole military-industrial family, no matter where they were.

Of course, we were responsible for putting the weapon system into the submarines. We also were responsible for the submarines. We were responsible for the submarines and everything that went into them. We were responsible for the supply ships, logistic spares and for the training of the weapon crews.

We worked directly with the Bureau of Ships but at first we were not working as well because we didn't have good lines of communication with them. So I went over to see the very wise then chief of the Bureau of Ships, Rear Admiral Al Mumma, who left the Navy at the end of his tour and became President and Chairman of the Worthington Corporation, and I told Al, whom I'd known for many years, that we were not working together as well as we could, and he said, "Well, what would you suggest?"

So I said, "I'd suggest that you get one of your rear admirals, a naval constructor, and order him down here and give him your authority in writing, so that the whole Bureau of Ships establishment, no matter where it is, will know that he is Mr. Polaris and he's exercising Chief of the Bureau's authority and has the Chief of the Bureau of Ships share or responsibility for the Polaris submarines. You all are going to build it. We're putting the weapon system into it, but you're going to build it." We had to fund everything that went into that submarine. The whole submarine was funded through my budget and, in effect, we were responsible for it.

He said, "That's a good idea." I said, "He'll set up a management center similar to ours, except yours will be devoted to your work, but it will be in consonance with ours so that we can speak to each other, and we'll know and you'll know how things are going, where the soft spots are and where the effort is." He said, "Have you got any ideas?" And I said, "Rear Admiral Jimmy Farrin comes to mind." So he said, "Well, you can pick 'em too. He's ideal, in my opinion, as your man." So Jimmy Farrin got telephone orders, dispatch orders, that same day to report bag and baggage without delay, which means immediately, to the office of the Chief of the Bureau of Ships, and he was given additional duty in my office, as my deputy for ships, for ship-building. So I fixed up an office that was even better than mine and bigger than mine and put him in it right next to my office. I said, "This is your office, Admiral, and you're my deputy now for the shipyards, the building of the ships, and the work of installing everything in the submarine. I'm looking to you to see that it gets done. My people will work with you and your people." I had a "ships" section which worked with me directly on my staff.

That turned out to be a very fine, excellent relationship and management technique. We didn't go in and try to give orders to the shipyard fellows, but we had one of their own admirals there who handled those duties for us. So what we did was utilize the existing chains of command to do the job. They knew the people, they knew how to do it, they knew it all far better than we did. And that was the same thing as we did in industry. We utilized their management and their management people to do the job, rather than going in and trying to tell them how to do the job, as is so much the case these days. That was a very happy arrangement.

Q: These were tremendous insights that you were acting upon.

Adm. R.: I don't call it an insight. It just seems to me like it's common sense. Who goes in the kitchen and tells your wife how to cook? Only a good cook, and I'm not a good cook. Not being burdened with a great deal of knowledge about anything, I just depend on a lot of people to do the work for me. It was a pet saying of mine that I would never do anything if I could get somebody else to do it for me, and I really used this principle. It was well quoted and well known. I would never do anything if I could get somebody else to do it because, one, the other fellow probably knew how to do the job far better than I, and two, it gave me time to do the things that only I could do. It gave me time to think. It' gave me time to look at the soft spots, the soft spots in performance or in part of our military-industrial team or soft spots in protecting our political lines in Washington. It gave me time to go and do something about it. That's why I had a good deputy. My deputy ran my show - the deputy and the chief civilian and the technical director were known as the "Board of Directors." Do you think I attended the Board of Directors? Hell, no! I didn't want to get into minutiae.

Q: The technical director was Levering Smith?

Adm. R.: It turned out to be Levering Smith.

Q: Tell me about his selection.

Adm. R.: He came on the scene at the change-over from the Jupiter to the solid-propellant motored missile. Our first technical director was a Bureau of Aeronautics man, who was a very fine gentleman, and he was quite talented - his name was Captain Grayson Merrill and he was a very fine technical man but not particularly knowledgable in large solid-propellants technology.

In my tour in the Bureau of Ordnance, which was during the Korean War some years previous, I became acquainted with Levering Smith who was then a lieutenant commander at the Naval Ordnance Test Station, Inyokern. He was in charge of solid rocket work out there. He came into my office one day with plans for a shaped-charge head which would fit on the 5-inch HVR rocket, which was an air to air rocket. (Aircraft against aircraft).

This shaped charge was a technique of pinpointing the explosive and directing it direct in a straight line and sort of funneling it against the target rather than having it going in all directions, as a normal explosion does. It's a very fine technique that optimizes the effect on a relatively small area.

Q: It focuses!

Adm. R.: Yes, focuses, exactly. We didn't have any rockets that would knock out those Korean tanks. These 5-inch HVR rockets had a fragmentation head which was designed to knock down aircraft. The result was there was a big hue and cry, why don't we have a shaped-charge head. Well, the shaped-charge head for that application was, by gentleman's agreement, in the hands of Army ordnance Department and at the time, because they didn't fly combat airplanes at that time, Army ordnance were not much interested in this. They had priorities elsewhere.

But Levering Smith and his cohorts out in Inyokern said, well, why don't we put a shaped-charge head on 5-inch rockets which would be carried by airplanes and aimed at the tanks. He presented himself with this idea and in those days a mere naval captain could start such a program by just merely giving the word. So I told him to go back with the utmost priority and develop this shaped-charge head for the 5-inch rocket. Then I sat down and wrote out a TWX and sent it to him, confirming it.

Within ten days' time they had fabricated this and fired it at a slab of ship armor, which was $17\frac{1}{2}$ inches of homogeneous armor - it had penetrated $17\frac{1}{2}$ inches of homogeneous armor which was at an angle of 75° from the horizontal, using a door-bell button for initiator so that they'd have the necessary stand-off position. The door-bell triggered off the mechanism, the shaped-charge was focused, and boomed right through and penetrated it. Well, they came dashing back to Washington with that news. That, of course, was a tremendous breakthrough, so the Chief of the Bureau of Ordnance was delighted with this, heartily applauded it, and told them to go ahead and hand-build as many as they could, and when they had a plane load there was an Air Force plane, which was an R-4D, waiting to fly the load directly to Korea.

That was my introduction to Levering Smith. He was quite an authority on solid propellants. So when it became evident we were going to go into solid propellants for motors, I brought him in, even though we had Captain Merrill there. Shortly after that Captain Merrill decided he would retire from the Navy of his own volition.

Q: No trips to Europe or anything!

Adm. R.: Captain Merrill had a boat lying in the Chesapeake and he went down there and played around on that boat for two weeks, and he decided that he was going to get out and go into civilian life. I, of course, was appalled by this and told him, "You've just queered two weeks leave for anybody else. I'll never give anybody two weeks to think about their troubles." One week, max!

So, when Levering Smith came on board, I said, you're the technical director, go to work. So, he went to work. He's a very dedicated and intelligent and I think he's the best scientist in uniform today. There's no question about it in my mind. He's dedicated, thorough, extremely wise. He and I would usually closed up the shop around seven or seven thirty.

I'd start home and go by his office and he'd be there working, and my invariable greeting was, "What's the matter? Did somebody forget to wake you up? It's time to go home." He'd grin and go on working.

But he, I think, has proved himself to be the finest scientist manager in uniform and he is, I guess, probably the most respected by the military and industry - technical officer, in my time. I don't know anyone who approaches him. Now, there have been some very good ones, there's no question about that, but I believe that over the years he has gained this enviable niche. It was a very happy thing for me to have a man like him - a very happy thing for the program and for our country.

Q: How did you happen to involve somebody like Jack Dunlap?

Adm. R.: Dunlap and I had collaborated when I was - I told you earlier that they got me back from World War II for one year in Washington to establish the aviation gunnery training program for the whole Navy, and Dunlap, an industrial psychologist, was then in uniform as a lieutenant commander in the Chief of the Bureau of Medicine and Surgery's office. I needed people who knew how to intelligently conduct tests to analyze the worthwhileness of this training equipment via a vis that training equipment. What it would do, so that you could teach a person aerial gunnery using machines on the ground. We had to use a lot of simulation machines to teach people because we couldn't afford to use the regular equipment and we wanted to have something that could be evolved in short order and get it in place in the numerous schools that we had established or were establishing.

So I called over there and got hold of a doctor friend of mine who was a psychologist who I thought might be helpful, and he said, "Yes, we have some very good people over here. They are Reserves brought back on active duty." So he sent Dr. Dunlop over, who has a Ph.D. in math and a Ph.D. in psychology, which is quite a combination - an ideal man because he knew a lot about controlled testing and he had great initiative. He used my authority and my name with considerable effect, going in and seeing the Commander in Chief, Atlantic, and saying, "Captain Raborn in the office of the CNO for Operations has asked this test to be run and I'd like a squadron of planes." "We're going down to Florida and we're going to do this, that, and the other - we're going to test this gun sight or that piece of equipment, and so on and so forth." He was amazingly efficient and brazen!

In the Polaris program it occurred to us that one of the real things that we had to explore and break ground in, was the adaptation of man to the machine. We were going to bring into existence machines and equipment which the Navy had not seen before, had no experience with. The necessity for the maintainability of the equipment aboard the submarine by the people aboard the submarine and the operability of the equipment by the personnel, was very high on our worry list. We wanted to optimize the knowledge of the people to maintain it and to make the equipment easy to maintain, make it self-diagnostic for trouble shooting as much as we could. To make it easily repairable and easily maintainable, because space aboard submarines is quite limited, as you know, and we wanted to put aboard spare parts and replacement parts for the equipment only to the extent absolutely necessary, because we just wouldn't have room for it. Something else had to "give", for everything we put aboard.

I asked Dr. Dunlap, who headed up his own firm, Dunlap and Associates, if he would like to take on a job of human engineering for the whole program. He was delighted and said, "This is the kind of thing I just love to do." So I said, "All right," and I gave him a letter that delegated my authority to him. He had authority to go into all of our principal contractors that were building these odd, weird and wonderful pieces of equipment and set up human engineering divisions that had absolute authority over how things were made as to their maintainability and operability by our naval personnel. So he had human engineering staffs in these various major companies, because he said there are a lot of guys running around with a human engineering title that he wouldn't let in the front door, much less do the work. So he had to staff them with competent people.

As it turned out, years later when the Defense Department just couldn't believe the high "up time" that the weapon system was consistently turning in on station, they sent out a very smart intelligent group of technical analysts to ride herd and see if these reports that the weapon system was completely operable and "ready" the very high portion of time on station were actually true. They came back with their hats in their hands. It was actually true.

The Navy evolved this system of pulling the sub off the line on signal as they would get in wartime, fire the missiles into a designated area, a realistic test. DOD would have people there to observe the efficiency of the tests. They were excellent! So I have to give Dr. Dunlap and his people a real plus in making the weapon system ready to go all the time, and, of course, that's the name of the game. He had at that time (during development of the system) my priority and he worked at this. I'm sure that he and his people got in the hair of the engineers, "any old dumb cluck ought to be able to do this, that, and the other thing", but he said never mind about that we will not be using highly trained scientific engineers with PhDs on the submarines. We must make the equipment simple and easy to maintain and to operate. Rugged!

Q: This, too, I suppose, was entirely new to the industries?

Adm. R.: Yes, I believe it was, particularly this amount of attention on human engineering, this emphasis, and we made a lot of todo about this, so that in the Polaris schools and so forth training was simplified. And well it was for the Polaris system in not childs play. At first we didn't have actual weapon system equipment for our schools, but I fought like a tiger and got the money and set up a school at Dam Neck, Virginia with actual weapon system equipment. We built it out of whole cloth, new buildings, new everything, and I'm embarrassed to say they named the building after me. I said you have to be dead to get that kind of an award and they said, not in this case.

Anyway, this school has a complete Polaris/Poseidon weapon system. The actual equipment is there and it's grouped by sub-systems in classroom sizes - here is the navigation system, here is the missile guidance, here is the fire-control system, and here is this, that, and the other - and here's the launcher. An actual launcher is out there - a couple of launchers and they can fire dummy loads in the air.

So the people coming back off patrols and those people coming new into the program go through this extensive training at Dam Neck, Virginia, and they operate the same equipment in the same way as they will aboard the submarine, and it is a rule that any new piece of equipment going to be introduced into submarines at sea - I'm talking about the weapon system now - first has to go to Dam Neck before it goes out into use in submarines. Because we want the people to be trained in it. The only real fight I ever had with that great gentleman Mr. Franke, Secretary of the Navy Franke, was when he wanted to cut me 50 million dollars - I asked for 100 million for the school and he cut it in half. I argued with him and argued with him and argued with him. I'd come back and he'd throw me out of the office. He said, "You're the hardest man to say no to that I've ever seen. I've thrown you out of my office three times and here you come right back."

I said, "Well, I can't let you make this mistake. This is a huge mistake." "Well," he said, "I'm going to make it. I've got to make one in this program" or something like that! So he whacked me 50 million dollars. I laughed. I said, "Well, okay, if you want to make one mistake, you can for you have been such a tremendous help and supporter of the program."

But he turned right around on the next year budget and made it up, so we were about six months late doing all the things we wanted to do, but we got them done. There isn't anybody who knows anything about the program at all who would say that that approach of putting the actual equipment in the school isn't absolutely essential. I must say Sec Franke was funny, a great man and a great supporter. I couldn't have worked for a finer man.

Q: Tell me how Clement Hayes Watson got involved in your program?

Adm. R.: At the very outset, of course, it was extremely important that we always in our contacts with other people present our ideas in a rational, effective way - "what" we were going to do, "why" do you want to do it, in our presentations or whatever they were. Somebody put a little pamphlet on my desk which was issued by the Chief of Naval Personnel on how to make a presentation. I read it and was quite interested. I immediately saw that this was really the work of great skill and wisdom and whoever wrote that for the Chief of Naval Personnel really knew his business. It just went home like that. So I said who was the man who authored this? Well, his name was Watson. Where does he live? In Connecticut, what is his phone number? They didn't know but they knew where he lived, so I called him on the phone and I said, "Mr. Watson, I'm calling in regard to one of the highest priority programs in the United States. We need your skills in teaching us to be effective in our presentations. Could you come down and talk to us about helping us?" And he said, "I will, certainly," and he came down the very next day.

He was a Reserve naval officer in World War II -

Q: He was no longer with J. Walter Thompson?

Adm. R.: No, he was running his own firm. He came down and I told him what we were doing and he said, "Gee, I'd be happy to," so we put him under contract. We required all of our officers and men - officers and civilians - at the home office to take this course on how do you prepare your materials and how do you talk and make an effective presentation.

Q: Sort of a Dale Carnegie set-up!

Adm. R.: Exactly, and he was very efficient. In fact, I sent him out to our principal contractors. He offered his services and was recieved quite well by them. We've got to give him a a lot of credit for the effectiveness of our presentations.

Q: This "road show" that you put on, he was --

Adm. R.: That was being put on by a lot of our people at all times, everyone, and we brought in what we called technical information officers who, in effect, were PRs, public information. They were very, very good. As a matter of fact, one of them turned up to be Deputy Chief of Naval Information. I think I gave you his name - Ken Wade. He currently runs the State of California's office here in Washington. He got me down and gave me some practice about mannerisms and so forth. "I noticed when you were talking you had a matchbox you were bouncing around," he said, "you know, that was very distracting for the people. You ought to stop things like that." And I said, thank you very much.

Effective presentations were, I think a very helpful element in the total result, getting the total job done.

Q: It's interesting, Sir, that you had this appreciation of the value of public relations and pursued it. This aspect of Navy life has not always been paramount. How do you account for that?

Adm. R.: I don't know. Of course, I'd had two tours of duty in Washington before - or three tours, or something like that - so I was not unacquainted with the way you have to get things done in Washington, the people that you had to contact, the people you have to convince that what you want to do is proper, correct, and needed, and get people to have confidence in you.

Q: But the Navy was rather reticent about this, wasn't it?

Adm. R.: I think most naval officers spend a lot of their time at sea, and I was one of those, but being first in battleships and destroyers then in aviation, I had more time, at sea, duty than actually anybody else in my admirals class. I think that statement is correct. But the importance of being able to present these things well and to get to the general public with our story - because there was a great deal of gee-hawing between the services. Each thought their own missile programs were the best for the country, and that's proper, there's nothing wrong with that opinion. That's a reality. Each of them had their supporters, their own associations and Navy Leagues or whatever you call them, and people as a whole across the United States were interested in this program. It was new and imaginative, something like the moon program when it first started. The result was that none of our officers once turned down an invitation to make a speech. I encouraged our officers to make speeches. They carried the Gospel, so to speak, about how important Polaris was, because a submarine goes out there and loses itself in the so-called trackless wastes of the ocean, yet always be ready to go, zeroed in and pinpointed on the target.

Without pointing the finger at land-based installations, we did, I think, in due fashion bring out before congressmen and others the advantage of the submarine approach to the ballistic missile defense.

Q: That was your party line!

Adm. R.: Yes, Sir. We never spoke badly about anybody or any other program. We made a policy of this, and it paid us big dividends. We had something to sell and why knock the other and maybe competitive products. We held the view, rightly or wrongly, publicly that we were not in competition with land-based missiles. We were providing sea-based missiles, and you shouldn't think of them in the same terms. They were a natural adjunct - strong adjunct - of the over-all national missile program. The contractural family in their normal PR work showed how proud they were of being on the team.

This was very, very helpful. As a matter of fact, I have several plaques. When I left the program they had a luncheon for me, all the PR types were there. Of course, they were all extroverts and great guys and they gave me a silver plaque containing a couple of silver spurs mounted on the plaque! Somebody said they wanted to put a little blood on it, but they thought better of it - a little red paint or something! This is the kind of total dedication you've got to have, and this was symbolic.

Q: The fact that you put great emphasis, and so rightly, on

public relations leads me to ask you about the matter of security. Was there any great concern in that area in the development of these sensitive matters?

Adm. R.: Security, yes. We were concerned about security in two ways. One, safeguarding valuable blueprints of innovative things which we were developing and bringing into existence. We had a fire once in a blueprint vault, a secure classified vault, at Lockheed. It was caused by a lamp that was too close to some blueprints. Fortunately they were able to put that fire out, otherwise we would have lost a lot of valuable time because many of these valuable, one copy of a kind, blueprints were in that vault. It was a huge vault. Instantly I was on the phone to Gene Root and I said, "I want you to establish two other repositories of blueprints. Whenever you make a blueprint, you make it at least in triplicate for stowage, make three copies, and I want you to stow it at two other places, secure, classified, top secret. When it comes off the machine, one goes in your vault and the other two go to two separate vaults, and none of them in the same city."

Q: Not in the same city?

Adm. R.: Not in the same city. There was such a thing as sabotage. Obviously this was a very important program and we didn't want someone throwing an incendiary bomb in there and, gee, it would throw us back two or three years developing the missile. So these were the kind of precautions we took.

As far as handling classified materials, we just applied the normal precautions, and the dedication of the people out on the factory floor and elsewhere to this program precluded a serious leak. If there was anyone against this program he would have been mobbed instantly by his fellow workers, you see.

Q: For the most part it was not secret except for the atomic aspect of it?

Adm. R.: Oh, no. All of the weapon system, navigational equipment, etc., was quite secret, quite classified. No one had ever done this before and obviously it behooved us to protect it. No one had ever built a stable guidance table for a missile that could be fired from under water, the motors igniting after coming through the water, and the missile then on its way to hit a target. No one had done that. No one knew about the launchers. The launch equipment was secret. The missile itself was secret. The formulation of propellants, how do you bind it, how do you put it in the motors, how do you keep it from cracking, and all that was quite secret. These were military assets of the first order.

Q: Were there any leakages?

Adm. R.: I don't know of any, but obviously as time went on, why, I'm sure that the exchange of technical information and things that could be declassified, a great majority of things that we did were declassified. That's all right. I mean that's a normal thing.

Q: That's evolution.

Adm. R.: Yes, that's right. It's just the normal thing that goes on in the technical world all the time. There's nothing wrong with it at all.

Polaris - a story of dedicated government-military-industry cooperation working in a free society, and free from excessive bureaucracy, developed out of whole cloth a revolutionary weapon system in an unprecedented short time, fully operational and on station, in little over four years!

There's a lesson in this program for someone today. But can we turn back the tide of ever enlarging bureaucracy in military procurement?

DECLARATION OF TRUST

The undersigned does hereby appoint and designate as his (her) Trustee herein, the Secretary-Treasurer and Publisher of the United States Naval Institute to perform and discharge the following duties, powers, and privileges in connection with the possession and use of a certain taped interview between the undersigned and the Oral History Department of the United States Naval Institute.

1. Classification of Transcript.

   (✓)a. If classified OPEN, the transcript(s) may be read or the recording(s) audited by the qualified personnel upon presentation of proper credentials, as determined by the Secretary-Treasurer of the U. S. Naval Institute.

   ( )b. If classified PERMISSION REQUIRED TO CITE OR QUOTE, the user will be required to obtain permission in writing from the interviewee prior to quoting or citing from either the transcript(s) or the recording(s).

   ( )c. If classified PERMISSION REQUIRED, permission must be obtained in writing from the interviewee before the transcribed interview(s) can be examined or the tape recording(s) audited.

   ( )d. If classified CLOSED, the transcribed interview(s) and the tape recording(s) will be sealed until a time specified by the interviewee. This may be until the death of the interviewee or for any specified number of years.

2. It is expressly understood that in giving this authorization, I am in no way precluded from placing such restrictions as I may desire upon use of the interview at any time during my lifetime, nor does this authorization in any way affect my rights to the copyright of my literary expressions that may be contained in the interview.

Witness my hand and seal this 1st day of February 1974.

Arleigh Burke

I hereby accept and consent to the foregoing Declaration of Trust and the powers therein conferred upon me as Trustee:

Interview with Admiral Arleigh Burke, U. S. Navy (Retired)

Place: His office in Washington, D.C.

Date: Tuesday morning, 19 September 1972

Subject: Polaris Project

By: John T. Mason, Jr.

Q: I suppose an outsider, Sir, could observe that the development of the Polaris was the crowning achievement of your whole period as CNO. At least, that's the way I feel as I review the whole thing.

Would you begin by talking about the situation vis-a-vis the missile and its development as you came into office in 1955?

Adm. B.: Yes, but I'm not so sure the Polaris was the best thing that happened. It was very good, but there were a lot of other things, too, that were quite important, things that could, and may be will, have long-range implications.

I was a very junior rear admiral when I was appointed and I didn't really want the job very much - I didn't want it at all, as a matter of fact - at that time. I wasn't very ambitious and I was very much concerned, the way I am concerned now, that the officials of the government felt that the Navy did not have good line officers who could become CNO who were senior to me, because obviously there was something wrong with the Navy training, if that were true. This bothered me than. It bothers me now. There were good people senior to me who would have been good CNOs. They could have filled the job, and because there was lots of experience that I had not yet had, and I wanted the experience of command of fleets before I became CNO, if I were to become CNO, and I didn't much care whether I did or not. Not because it's a hard-working job. I didn't mind that, but because there are a lot of other jobs that are of nearly equal importance and I didn't like the continual fights you had to have. They weren't really fights, but explanations to Congress, the Bureau of the Budget, and everybody.

Q: The political overtones!

Adm. B.: The political overtones were the thing. Anyway, when I talked to Mr. Thomas, the Secretary of the Navy, he said, yes, they'd been looking around but there were a lot of things that he was dissatisfied with. The Navy was too slow in adopting a lot of new ideas, mostly in weapons systems. He felt that what they needed was somebody who would make these advances reasonably and who would generate support for them. There were lots of divisions in the Navy, as there always are in a big organization, and they had decided, and it was too late to change, that I should be it.

Well, that was very complimentary and I was very honored. It was also a hell of a lot of hard work ahead. I knew that. And I wasn't so sure that all of Mr. Thomas' ideas were ones I agreed with, particularly on personnel and particularly on young personnel - on putting young personnel into positions of great responsibility, which is all right at times, but it's not a good policy because you don't get the experience in the senior ranks. Also the government, the Navy, pays for a man all of his life and then doesn't use him in the most productive times of his life, which are after he has had the experience and gotten the wisdom and made his mistakes. The Navy could profit by those mistakes. At the same time I recognized that there was some dead wood, as there is in all big organizations, all big governmental organizations.

Anyway, I was appointed and around the 1st of June I came down here for about two months before I was to take office. I made a list of all the problems that confronted the Navy that I could find. I talked to lots and lots of people. I listed them, one problem, one page. Many of them seemed unsolvable, many of them were personnel, many of them were weapons systems, many of them were connected with money, most of them had great differences of opinion within the Navy as well as outside of the Navy as to what should be done, how to solve these problems. But among them were the material things of weapons systems. Surface-to-air missiles were coming along then fairly well. I'd had some experience with surface-to-air missiles because I was in Research, BuOrd.

As I say, I made this list of problems.

Q: It must have been a formidable one!

Adm. B.: Yes, it was, and I ended up before I became CNO with categories of problems in books. I had about 50 notebooks, each one for a category of problems. For example, one category was "Army" - problems with the Army; another one was "Missiles,"; another one was "Torpedoes"; another one would be "Personnel - Promotion and Assignment." All kinds of categories, and I had people keep up those books after I'd become CNO for a while, so that they were condensed, and each time I read a page I initialed it. Each time there were significant changes, the lad who was responsible for that category would make the change and I'd have a page there that I'd not initialed, so I read one of those books every night - I'd go through it so that I kept current.

This thing of listing the problems started that sort of general procedure.

One of the big problems was the Air Force-Navy controversy over what has become known as strategic warfare, the delivery of nuclear weapons on an enemy territory. The Air Force was insistent that only they could do it, with SAC and with their tactical aircraft, but mostly SAC. Ballistic missiles were just commencing to come into being. The Army had a tremendous missile, but it had a short range, 200 miles - I've forgotten the name of it now (Jupiter), and the Air Force had an Atlas missile that they were working on, a ballistic missile, short-range, too, but longer than 200 miles.

I made an analysis of that problem. It may be some place in my files, probably in pencil. And I came to the conclusion that, sooner or later, if they could get a high specific impulse of a good fuel and could get a reasonably-sized warhead, ballistic missiles were going to replace aircraft for the delivery of large quantities of nuclear weapons. Also, in the same analysis, ballistic missiles from fixed bases were necessarily very vulnerable - three great big beasts sitting on a launching pad in those days were very vulnerable to a very little shock.

Q: And you couldn't keep it secret, the sites?

Adm. B.: You couldn't keep it secret. Everybody would know where they were, so that it would be very easy to knock them out.

So, I thought a mobile ballistic missile would have tremendous advantages. The Navy was the place that had the mobility and the equipment for mobility. I worked on this a little bit, and when I got a fairly good idea of what I thought could be done, I started to talk to people, mostly to our own missile people. At that time, the section was headed by Admiral Savvy Sides. The missile people weren't very eager to go into ballistic missiles, or to do any research on ballistic missiles.

Q: Why were they not?

Adm. B.: Money. It takes a lot of money and what good would these tremendous beasts be on ships? They were all liquid-fueled then, and because of that they were dangerous aboard ship as well as big, they would take a lot of research, and all that research, money, and effort would come from other programs, and there were lots of problems that we would have with a moveable missile that a fixed-base missile would not have, such as location, getting the exact location, navigational position. Also, which way is up. That was one of the hardest things that we had to figure out. How to compensate for roll and pitch, because it takes time for those missiles to get launched. There were tremendous numbers of problems.

Q: In spite of their reluctance, was there not some pressure from outside - the knowledge that the Russians were making progress?

Adm. B.: Not a damned bit.

Q: Really!

Adm. B.: Not a damned bit. Everybody now thinks that there was a lot of push behind these missiles, and there wasn't. People in the Navy pushing, but nobody outside of the Navy gave a damn or a thought or anything at all about a ballistic missile at sea that I ever heard of. I've heard of it since, but not then. Not then. And I got very little support for this idea. I realized that there were an awful lot of obstacles to that, and it didn't come full bloom, to build a ballistic missile for the Navy. I wanted to do research on it because, if it could be developed, it would be a weapon system that would be much less vulnerable and they would not have to have the ranges that intercontinental missiles do. People had thought of intercontinental missiles then, but they were still far away. They were not a sure thing at that time.

Q: Wasn't the White House alert to the fact that the situation was getting "hot"?

Adm. B.: Oh, no, no. There was nobody getting hot. Delivery of nuclear weapons was hot, yes - and intercontinental ballistic missiles was a hot subject, but nobody was interested in putting these things aboard ship, because the problems were terrible. There were great big problems. There were people inside the Navy - a few - who felt that it would be a good idea.

I talked to our strategy people, Op-03 (Op-06 people, in those days), to determine what they thought of a strategy, never mind the techniques of developing this missile, but could a strategy of ballistic missiles at sea be useful for the United States? Well, of course, it came back very easy. It would be very important for the Navy.

Q: Was this George Miller's idea also?

Adm. B.: George Miller wasn't in there then. No. I can't

remember who was in Op-03. Of course, there was no thought of submarines then, either, because you couldn't put a Jupiter in a submarine. It was a very large liquid-fueled missile. Nobody thought of submarines.

After a lot of discussion, I convinced a few people, and I said, "Let's see if we can't do this ourselves. There's no need for us to start our own missile because both the Air Force and the Army have done a lot of work on these missiles. Why don't we just join one of them?"

So I went to the Air Force and asked them, my good friend Nate Twining, and I went down to his research people, his missile people, and I said:

I want about a foot in your missile to put in the equipment that's going to be needed for a Navy missile, and we'll pay for it. We'll pay for part of your research. We'd like to buy into your program. With that foot I think we can get the things that will be needed for navigational corrections and other devices that we'll need at sea but you don't need ashore."

They thought it over about ten minutes, and said no, that it would complicate their R & D problem, that they wouldn't gain anything by it, they were doing very fine, and just, no soap.

Q: And this was a liquid propellant –

Adm. B.: Sure. These were all liquid propellants.

Then I went over to the Army, and the Army considered it,

and they finally said, all right, you pay for it and we'll give you a foot in the Jupiter missile.

Then I went to our missile people and said, "What can we mount this thing in? What can we do?" After a little bit of work - this was all within a couple of months - they decided we needed a great big hull. So we got an old aircraft tender and prepared it to mount a Jupiter missile. We could do this. It didn't take much money or time. But the next step was going to take a lot of money.

We worked very closely with the Army and the Army were very good to us. They helped us a great deal. The Air Force helped us, too. They didn't want us messing with their missile but they'd give us advice and they helped.

Q: This was all within the year 1955, was it?

Adm. B.: Yes, or very early 1956, but 1955 probably.

Q: It was before the Killian Committee came forth with their report?

Adm. B.: The Killian Committee came forth just about the time that we had gotten the preliminary things done. And all of this was informal. I mean it wasn't a question of great big contracts with the other services. It was all very informal.

Q: Was Wilson congnizant of the whole thing?

Adm. B.: Maybe not. It was not that big. I suppose he knew

about it. These things don't come full-born. It looks like they do afterwards, but originally they don't.

Well, we got along fairly well and we got ideas from a lot of people. Obviously, if it went forward, it was going to cost like hell. I was my own missile man on that for several months and I couldn't handle it and do anything else. I was paying an hour's attention a day, or less than that maybe, to it. But I wanted to get the concepts moving. So I wanted to find somebody to run it. We had the best missile men in the Navy in the missile division, or a lot of them. If this thing moved it had to have the complete support of a large number of organizations within the Navy, the Bureau of Ordnance, BuShips, BuAir. It had to have the support of large industrial research organizations. It had to have a tremendous amount of support. It couldn't be done by fear. You had to get people interested in it. So what we needed to head this organization was a man who could get other people to do a hell of a lot of work and had an idea of organizing his work and who could get things done without creating a fight and without going around and demanding things. We've had enough of - like Rickover, for example. That's all right as long as he's got research and development fairly well completed, but when you've got to go into a large research and development program, then you don't know what talents you're going to need so you've got to have people at the top who can get that talent by willing participation.

Burke - 11

I studied the flag list and I went over every flag officer every night. One of the things that I would do when I got home would be to go over that damned list, and I went over the list of captains. Who could it be? What kind of a man did you want? It always came back to, it would be nice if he had technical abilities, he had to have a good organizational ability - that had to be, he had to be a hard worker, he had to be persuasive, he had to be a salesman, he had to be able to separate the important things from the nonimportant things, and he had to know what he was doing.

Q: You termed him later an extraordinary man!

Adm. B.: Yes. There were a lot of people who were very good. It should be an aviator, because it was going to displace an aviation mission. Also there was a large number of aviation problems involved in building such a missile.

Finally, I selected Red Raborn, which turned out to be my big contribution. I told Red when he came in:

"You have the choice of any forty officers that you want in the Navy. You can pick any forty officers and they're yours, but you can't have forty-one."

Q: How did you select the magic number of forty?

Adm. B.: Because that's about as big an organization as one man can handle by himself. It's not a magic number, it was just pulled out of a hat. If I were starting it now, I wouldn't say forty. I would say twenty, because I've had some experience on the outside. Then I knew too - and I know it very well now - that Americans have one extremely bad habit, and that is they want to make massive mistakes, they want to cure all the problems of the world by one damned procedure, one solution. They aren't cured that way, and they get these great big massive organizations and they don't do anything.

Q: Empire-building!

Adm. B.: Yes, but they don't build them, they just create them all at once. This is what I think has largely happened to a lot of our social programs. You get incompetent people. You get people who are not hard enough worked. You get people you don't know very much, whose ideas are not suitable for the development of such a program.

Q: It's beyond the family concept, isn't it?

Adm. B.: Yes. That's why this organization that's here is small, it's compact, and it's always hungry. You have to have more than you can do in order to separate the trivia and not do the trivia.

Q: Did Raborn go along with this idea?

Adm. B.: Sure, he went along with it very well. He was enthusiastic about it. I told him that our big trouble was money, and that I had to know the status of this program all the time, adn he did too because he'd have to tell me. Once a week he'd have to come over and tell me where he stood. He had to devise some sort of a system so that he knew where he stood. I'd had a lot of research work in my life and this idea of non-duplication of research, I knew, was stupid. You've got to duplicate research. You could look back on a project and see where money was wasted on duplication _after_ you'd had a success. Then you could determine all the stuff you didn't need to have a success and, need not have been spent, if you knew what research would be successful in advance. But you don't know that in advance.

Q: You have to look at the different facets as you go along!

Adm. B.: Yes, that is right. Also, you have to develop down different ways. So I said, "Every time you run into a problem you get several different methods of attack on that problem by different groups, and you've got to stay within your budget. Whatever your budget is when you make it out the first time. We will do the best we can do, but don't try the camel's nose in the tent idea - get a little bit of money and then go for more. Let's make it as honest as we know how.

"Also, we have to have kill points in this thing."

Q: Why did you think of that precautionary measure - the kill points?

Adm. B.: Because the hardest thing to do -- and this has been emphasized both in the Navy and since I have retired - is to kill a program that isn't quite succeeding. People think if you could only solve this one problem, the rest of the program would go, and so you keep pouring money into programs that never work. It's very difficult to kill a program. Since then, I have found that the mark of a good businessman is to know when to stop, what not to do, where not to put his money because you can waste an awful lot of money on useless things that don't turn out. Not all of these things are going to turn out but when you've done enough research so that you've reached the stage where you don't have the answers and it doesn't work the way it is, the way you want it to, you can pour lots of money into trying to cure that, and it's a question of whether to do that or not. If you carry it along month by month, or quarter by quarter, or year by year, lots of times it never works.

This happens in civilian life, it happens everywhere, and this is one thing that you learn in research.

Anyway, Red picked this up. He got some of the best officers in the Navy. He went to work. He developed the PERT system. He had things under control. He had a lot of trouble. He didn't suddenly develop a system to do it. The system grew as he grew.

Q: You said later, in writing about it, that there were several times when it looked like the kill point was going to be reached. Would you elaborate on that?

Adm. B.: Well, we made major kill points, which we knew right away, but you can never tell when a little thing might cause you to be unable to accomplish what you intend to accomplish. It might be a very minor thing.

One of the major kill points was that we had to get a war head of a small size and small weight which would have a significant yield. We were shooting for one megaton and about 500 or 600 pounds, but we could accept a half-megaton and 500 or 600 pounds. In other words, we could give a little bit on the yield. What I guess I'm really saying is that we thought the weight was important. The yield was important, too, but there was some give in the yield.

We had to know the position of the ship, which we could not know with the techniques that we had then, very accurately. We had to be able to deliver within plus or minus, I think, three miles was the initial limit. CEP had to be three miles or less. We had to take care of the yaw and pitch. The guidance system was a kill point.

Also, we had to have a propulsion system that was reliable and not so dangerous as to jeopardize your ship every time you fired. There's danger in all of these things, but it had to be a reasonable amount of danger. You had to get a specific impulse which would lift this thing, lift the weight of the beast plus a warhead, to get a range of 1,500 miles because that's the geography of the Soviet Union and the seas around it.

Any one of those would have killed it, if we hadn't been able to make it, and we damned near didn't make it. AEC came through with their warhead, which was half a megaton and weighed about 600 pounds, and they thought they could refine it.

About that time I went over to see the Army. By this time, after Red had been there several months, things had to be codified. It was getting to be big, and it was going to cost a lot of money. I had to get the money, so I took money from other places, three other programs. Then it got so big I saw the SecNav, they were interested in it. I saw the Secretary of Defense, and they were interested in it, I saw their research people, they were interested in it.

Q: But not so generous with money!

Adm. B.: No, no. They said, "You furnish the money." We had to get this thing lined up so that people knew what we were doing and we had to have an agreement with the Army other than a gentlemen's agreement, a written agreement with the Army. Also, when Red had done a little work, it looked like it had a possible chance of success - not a probable chance, but it was possible that it might succeed, so other people wanted to get in the act. You have to get permission. One of the nice things about government service is that lots of people want to get in a position of power where they have to give the permission. They may not know a damned thing about what they're doing, but they want to give the permission to go ahead. It gives them a big feeling of authority. They do have authority. But this was not true

Burke - 17

with the informal agreement with the Army. They were damned good about that.

We had to codify that, so we got permission from the SecNav and got his support. And we got permission from SecDef and got his support, and they made all the agreements. The agreement with the Army said that we were searching for a solid-propellant ballistic missile with a light warhead that would have at least a half megaton yield and would be suitable for firing aboard ship, and as small a missile as possible to reach 1,500 miles.

Now, if we were able to get those characteristics, we would shift to solid propellant, and of course we had to have a solid propellant that had a specific impulse which would give 1,500 miles. If, at that time, the Army wanted to come along with us, that was fine, we'd like to continue the relationship, but we would divorce them if they didn't want to come along. We would go on our own.

Q: Is it not true that in the year 1956, at the request of the Secretary of Defense, the Navy did cooperate with the Army on Jupiter? This is where you put your main thrust?

Adm. B.: No, damnit, it was not at the request of the Secretary of Defense!

Q: Oh, it wasn't?

Adm. B.: No. That's what I've been telling you about it all

Burke - 18

along here. This thing started when I went over to see Trudeau in the Army - I think it was Trudeau - to ask them to go into it. When the Secretary of Defense got into it it was a long time after the initial work was being done, and then we started to codify it. That's the time when people want to get into it. The Army helped us out to beat hell, and we did an awful lot of work with the Army. We helped them some, too.

But it was not at the Seccetary of Defense's request, it was me going over and seeing Lemnitzer and saying - or Taylor, I guess it was: I'd like to go down and talk to your people in research." And I talked to Trudeau or his predecessor, and they said, sure, we'll go along with it.

Q: I'm glad to have that, Sir, because the written reports -

Adm. B.: Oh, sure, but how in God's name does the Secretary of Defense know how to direct something like that? He can't possibly know.

Q: I wondered myself.

Adm. B.: He can't possibly know. This is because somebody in the Secretary of Defense's office - well, it doesn't really matter very much, but proposals on weapons systems usually develop down the line from an idea. The man who has the idea discusses it with other people and then preliminary tentative proposals are submitted up the line. The top man very seldom, the CNO for example, usually does not originate the idea, but Polaris was one thing I did start. I started this thing. Very seldom did I start anything as CNO. Somebody suggested an idea

Burke - 19

or proposal and I supported it. 99 Percent of the proposals from CNO's office were somebody else's suggestion. And this is what happened with the SecDef. SecDef didn't know anything about ballistic missiles at sea until somebody told him. Mr. Wilson or his people didn't go around and say, "Now, look, we've got a bright idea. Let's have a Polaris submarine. We will develop it and do all these things." That's not the way weapons systems get formed. This is the way they've been trying to form them recently. This is the way Mr. MacNamara liked to form them, only nothing came out, and it doesn't come out because you cannot direct this from the top. You can't direct a schedule of invention. You can't direct how a man shall think or what he can think of.

This is why his F-14 failed. This is why a lot of the programs are in serious trouble now in the Navy and in other weapons systems too. It's because they're trying to direct it, possibly stemming from the fact that it was said that this is the way the Polaris started. It wasn't that way. It wasn't directed.

Q: I'm mighty glad you underscored that!

Adm. B.: This thing came about because the biggest asset that Red Raborn had was enthusiasm, the drive and enthusiasm to get it down. I told him, "If this thing works, you're going to be one of the greatest people that ever walked down the pike. You'll be a technical expert. If it fails, I'll have your throat." And he took it with that understanding.

Q: Guaranteed to lose sleep at night!

Adm. B.: No, it doesn't bother, because you do the best you can do, and that's all you can do.

But the formal things come out after a lot of informal work.

Let's go back to another weapons system. Let's take Sidewinder. Who the hell directed Sidewinder? This is typical of the way things develop. A young man (Maclean) out in a missile station in California got an idea that he could build an air-to-air missile, and so he built it. It was not very good to start with. It didn't work very well. It didn't cost very much either. But he couldn't get anybody interested in the damned thing because he couldn't prove it, and he couldn't get any money for it. So someone went out there and talked with him - I think it was one of Savvy Sides people who went, and he came back and said "this scoundrel might have something." He had the idea, and he probably got the idea from somebody else, too, he talked it over. You never develop it all by yourself, even he couldn't do that probably. But finally he was able to persuade a couple of people that it was a good idea. The missile station didn't think so much of it and didn't want to put it on their budget, so the missile people back here recommended that we give him a little bit of money. We did, and he developed the Sidewinder.

At that time, Sidewinder became an official beast. That's

when your official records start. But all of the preliminary work that this poor devil had done for two or three years was a long time before there was any official record.

The same thing is true with most any weapon system. Take radar. Radar was developed in many different countries at about the same time, but in this country it was developed by Dr. Page, I think, down in NRL. He was doing some work on radio and he had a radio set that he beamed across the Potomac, and when a ship went by - in those days ships went by on the Potomac - he got a peculiar reaction. Well, he didn't say: "Look, I've just invented radar!" He got a peculiar reaction and never thought anything of it. He did this for a couple of months, then he said: "This is an anomaly. Something happens."

Eventually, he changed his frequency, he fiddled around, and pretty soon he got a very crude system that could give him an indication and maybe a bearing, a rough bearing. He got a pretty good range and a very rough bearing.

Now, up until the time that Dr. Page comes in and says, look, I think I've got something here - and he had probably talked about it with all of his associates a long time before and they said "maybe you ought to try this, maybe you ought to lower the frequency, maybe you ought to get more power into the thing, maybe you ought to try a different kind of an antenna," he gets a lot of help. But until the time that he brings it up, "I think I've got something. I need some money to develop it, to find out whether I've got anything or not," nobody at the top knew about it.

This is the way it usually happens.

Q: That's the way it happened in England, too, isn't it, with Watson-Watt?

Adm. B.: Yes.

Now, there are exceptions to that, like the Mahattan Project., and there have been other exceptions. But still, most of the preliminary work is done, gathered by people a long time before they develop the organization to develop the weapon. The Mahattan Project was successful because they got every man in the Free World who knew a damned thing about nuclear things at all. They collected them all in one spot and then said, go to work and develop something, and they were able to do it.

But, to get back to Polaris. Then Red gave me his estimate, the money he needed, so I went over to see the Secretary of Defense and he said, "Let's see the Secretary of the Navy to get permission to reprogram." But that wasn't enough money. I wouldn't reprogram enough.

Q: How much were you thinking about?

Adm. B.: Oh, I don't know. A hundred million, maybe. Probably not that much, maybe fifty million. But SecDef said, "Fine, you can develop this, but you furnish the money -- can you re-program?

Take it out of the other Navy programs, if you think this is so damned good."

I said, "I don't think it's that good yet. I wasn't confident and it costs too much money for us."

He said: "Well, then, drop it. If you want to try it, you pay for it." So I said, "If I can reprogram it and if it is successful and if I drop 15,000 people out of the Navy to get the money, will you give the money back to me next year, if it's successful."

"Yes."

So that's what I did. The way we got the first money was to drop 15,000 people.

Q: That must have had a lot of headaches in itself!

Adm. B.: It did. And then we reprogramed a lot of other money from other sources, but still the opposition to this program within the Navy was very sound because what I was doing was exactly what they told me I was going to have to do. I would take a lot of money from other programs that needed it very badly to put into something that I wasn't sure was going to work.

Q: And the other programs were ongoing ones?

Adm. B.: They were ongoing ones. And they said, "You will wreck the Navy if you go too far."

Well, this was true, true as hell if it didn't work.

Q: That was an awful thought to live with.

Adm. B.: But is was true. But every time you do anything of any importance, you have to measure the consequences of what you have to gain versus the risks, and you have to measure it as accurately as you know how, and you can't avoid it without dire consequences.

Another American trait is that we're optimistic. Everything is going to be lovely. If we could just get started, everything is going to be lovely. And it will always work. Well, it doesn't always work. You have to face these risks realistically, but once you can face them realistically, then you know damned well that if this thing fails you've done a great deal of harm, so you don't want it to fail. And you don't nurse it along. You've got to make it go. Or you've got to kill it.

Q: Something of a scientific gambler you have to be?

Adm. B.: You have to. To do any research at all, you have to do that. You take a scientist, a lad who graduates, gets his Ph.D., say, and goes into a research laboratory, he can choose one of two ways. He can go under the direction of an experienced scientist and do what he's told to do in little jobs that will reach out a little bit, and he will be secure and, if he works hard, his position will be secure. But if in the back of his head he's got an idea that he can get power from the sun, and if we're in, say now, a great energy crisis and we've got to get energy and there's a lot of energy in sunshine - that's been tried before - but he wants to work on that.

Well, he's got to figure out in his own mind whether or not the prospects of his being successful if he devotes his entire time to getting power from the sun, or, say, 50 percent of his time. If he's successful, he will be a great man. He will have accomplished a great thing. But if he is not successful, he's going to end up in the back room of some laboratory, as a crank. And there are lots of them.

You have to take risks. You have to analyze the project and this is why you have kill points. You have to make sure that you re-evaluate the project all the time. What do you do if something starts to go wrong? This is what Mr. MacNamara did not do. He was a great man to say that he would have a lot of options, he would choose his course of action from a lot of options, and he would determine the course of action he would take from all the courses of action he could get. But, what he did <u>not</u> do was to say "After I have chosen this course of action and we start going down that road, what shall I do if something goes wrong, if it isn't right? Do I shift to another course of action? Do I kill it? What do I do?"

This is not what he did. When he made the F-111, he chose the course of action which he thought was the best one initially, but he didn't deviate from that. He never looked at it to see how it was going. How are we doing today? Are we making improvements? Is it going to work? What do we do if it does go wrong?

Take the development of the F-4. The F-4 is the best airplane that the United States has yet, probably. But the F-4 was one of two airplanes - the F-4 and the F-8 were two parallel approaches to accomplish exactly the same thing, to get one good fighter airplane. They both turned out to be pretty good airplanes, but the F-4 was the better one. The initial risk we reduced greatly by going after two. It cost money, but over-all, it cost a lot less money than having one failure and nothing to back you up.

So, in a thing like this Polaris missile, you're taking a great risk because these were hundreds of millions of dollars at that time, and the development of that meant that you cut back on other programs, You hurt the Navy.

Q: I suppose, Sir, another way of saying it is that you have to have the courage to make the effort, but you also have to be possessed of a certain amount of humility to admit that you made a mistake if you have?

Adm. B.: You have to have alot of advice, a lot of people to help you. This is where the Navy's very fortunate. They have a lot of people to help, if you ask, but you have to weigh it yourself and see what the risk is that you're taking, and the most important thing is who do you put, not to try to solve the problem, but who do you put in your organization to make it go. One thing that I learned as CNO is that you could never give an order. The CNO cannot give an order. If he does, he ruins his organization, as is commencing to be found out now.

What you do if you have an idea that you would like to be put into effect is find somebody in that line of work and talk it over with him. Maybe he gets enthusiastic about it. If so, you put him in charge. He can follow through, you cannot. He puts it through and he develops it. But he's got to know that if this thing is not going to work or he thinks it's not going to work, he's got to come back and kill it. He's either got to have you kill it or he's got to kill it himself, because not everything works, as I found out, such as the Seamaster.

The Polaris success is due, primarily, to Red Raborn and the people he chose, because he made it work.

Q: Also to your concept of the Special Projects Office, which was out and beyond the others.

Adm. B.: Yes, but that again has been abused. That is a parasitic office. It's a parasite. It lives on the life blood of other organizations.

Q: They have to be in existence!

Adm. B.: They have to be in existence, they have to be competent. and they have to have enough blood so that you can take out some of it and support a parasitic organization. One organization like that you can handle, you may be able to handle two, but you can't handle six, because there isn't that much blood in your organization.

This project worked beautifully. It was perfect, because there was only one. So they start making little Polaris projects all around and they've got project officers that have these same characteristics. Well, they can't do it because the Bureau of Ordnance, the Bureau of Ships, and BuAir don't have that much talent, that much blood, they can't divert their efforts that much. You've got to have a standard, dull, routine organization, then you can have a little parasitic organization on it to bleed hell out of it. But you can't have two or three because you don't know where to direct the blood, where to direct the effort. This is the organizational knowledge you get when you run a boy scout troop, but a lot of people don't have it. And this is true in civil life.

I just read in The Wall Street Journal yesterday about Mr. White, who had all these wonderful ideas and when he was 26 he formed a big conglomerate and, at 32, he was all finished. He destroyed a lot of good people along with himself and he failed. He was all finished simply because he violated some fundamental rules of getting things done.

Q: Apparently he did, yes.

Adm. B.: He was a big white hope, but he didn't have the experience, or the knowledge, or the wisdon, or the humility. He thought he knew it all.

Q: In giving Admiral Raborn this authority to draw from all the bureaus and so forth, did you run into any initial problems with bureau chiefs?

Adm. B.: No. I told them that Red could have anybody, and there was no problem. This is a remarkable thing. Red had no trouble with any bureau chief. I didn't have any trouble with any bureau chief, but they warned me about the possible dangers, which they should have done. They didn't like it sometimes, and they had good reasons not to like it. But once they were asked to do it, they did it wholeheartedly. They put their whole heart into it. This is what made the Polaris successful, not just Red. You've got to have more than a good leader. You've got to have good support.

Q: He stresses the team nature of the thing.

Adm. B.: Sure. There were an awful lot of very fine people who did everything they possibly could to help this, not because they believed in it, but because they knew that if any system was going to work it needed that kind of enthusiastic support.

Another thing here, you can't get too many of these projects going at once, because you can't divide your enthusiasm into too many small parts.

Q: At that stage of the game, Sir, were there some pressures from outside? I mean, was there then an awareness within the administration and the government that we had to get on with this project?

Adm. B.: As soon as Red got busy and started contacting companies, yes, there was enthusiasm, but there wasn't any pressure, or at least not much pressure. There were a lot of people who were enthusiastic about it, but nobody was directed. Nobody was saying "this must be done," except within the Navy and Red himself.

Q: At that point, what was the attitude of the Congress?

Adm. B.: Congress was about the same as SecDef - OK - because we didn't get any money for a year. We took it out of the Navy's hide. The next year we got some money, when it looked fairly successful.

Congress always is and should be very skeptical. They should be very, very skeptical. They have appropriated money time after time to useless projects. Some times they have had people get up there and lie in their teeth before Congress. More often, they've had a lot of very earnest enthusiastic people get up there and say "this is what will happen." They appropriate the money and it doesn't happen. They've had a lot of experience and they're very skeptical.

When we went up there on Polaris, we tried not to overstate. It's a good weapon system. If it works it may be wonderful, but we've got to have money to find out whether it can work or not, and they gave it to us, after a year or so, because we had put up our own money first. We had suffered. Let's take another subject there and one that's completely different.

Vinson Hall over here is a home for widows, Navy widows. No money. It needs 5 or 6 million dollars to make this thing self-supporting. It's got to be raised. Who raises it? You can't get that much money from Navy people, but unless the Navy people themselves contribute heavily to that, you cannot in good conscience go to any outsider and say, please give me $100,000 to help Navy people. You can't do it. The Navy's got to do it itself. Congress reacts that way, too, and so does everybody else. If the Navy people do do this, you can get money from the outside, but if the Navy people don't do that, you won't. And with Congress, if the Navy is willing to take this risk itself and do this at the great expense to its other programs as it had, they believe in it, and they will trust your belief. Not that they can determine whether or not it's really a good program, they have to determine who's behind it, because they don't have that kind of knowledge.

Q: Did they offer any objections to Admiral Raborn's system of going outside the ordinary channels and making contracts with industry without bids and all that sort of thing?

Adm. B.: No.

Q: They saw the wisdom of that, did they?

Adm. B.: Well, you go up and explain. I made a lot of trips to the Hill. I'd go up and just talk about these things. How it's going to be done. So did Red. No, there wasn't any serious opposition. There's always the question, though, of corruption when you start going outside channels - not so much corruption, as stupidity. Somebody makes a big mistake and you don't know it. Channels have been developed because people have made mistakes in the past, and from their mistakes a system is developed.

Q: So, here, personal integrity on your part and on Raborn's part were essential to the Congress?

Adm. B.: It helped. Not just those two, but a lot of people with personal integrity and a lot of people with good judgment. You've got to trust not only the man's intent, because there are an awful lot of people with the best intent in the world that you couldn't have do anything because they don't know how, but also his skill. Red is a skillful man and he had some very good people working with him, and he had some very good support all over. These companies also put everything they had into it. That's the only program I know of that met its initial budget, stayed within its initial budgets from beginning to end. You had to do that to create credibility, so that people will trust you, not because you say "you've got to trust me," but they trust you because you have proved yourself to be trustworthy.

Q: They stayed within their budget and at the same time they beat the time schedule?

Adm. B.: They beat the time schedule. One of the things that we decided was that I'd add 10 percent to that budget for inflation. You're not supposed to add for inflation. You're supposed to take it on current dollars - estimates on current dollars - at least then. But inflation was here then too, and you underestimate. We were very conservative on all of our estimates so that instead of taking the very minimum, we would take a reasonable figure plus a little, so that we were sure we could operate within it, pretty sure that we could operate within it. You can't do that all the time.

Our time schedules, our money required, the talent required, and things like that, we tried to overestimate just a little bit to make sure we were sound, and it turned out to be about right. This was due to Red and his people that we were able to do that. It was not due to anybody else.

Q: How much interest did President Eisenhower show in this program as it went along?

Adm. B.: Initially, none at all, but as it went along he got very much interested in it and was very much in favor of it. He supported it. He was very good. He didn't get in on it at the beginning, of course, but he got in on it pretty soon.

Q: Admiral, why not talk about the successful results of this tremendous effort? On July 20, 1960, the first missile was successfully launched, a 1,200-mile missile.

Adm. B.: Well, that was, of course, a period of elation.

Q: Three and a half years after the project had begun!

Adm. B.: Yes. It was a wonderful thing that they did - for Red and his people to do.

Of course, as CNO I was elated and happy. This was something that really worked. It was very good. But from that time on it was a question of improvement. We knew that basically it could be done, so from that time on the problem was not a serious one for me. I'd got other problems. You had a lot of other things to devote your attention to.

Q: As you did all along, actually!

Adm. B.: Yes, you have to do this all along, and after a thing is successful you don't follow it as closely as you did before. I think this is natural. I know this works in the refineries now or in construction work. I'm on a mining project. We found copper, way in the interior of West Irian, ninety miles from the coast, in tropical jungle, impossible to get to. The technical problems are terrific, but we've solved those problems now. They are about to get the ore out now. Now it's not nearly as fascinating!

Q: Overwork worth the challenge!

Did Admiral Sides have anything to do with the initial efforts in this area?

Adm. B.: Oh, yes, he did. He and his group were the first people I talked to about the possibility of this sort of a system, and his group, largely, were opposed to it initially for very good reasons. They had problems enough with the surface-to-air missiles and their guided missiles. But after the decision was made they rallied round and helped very much. They were my contact with Red Raborn's outfit on technical things. They were a great help to Raborn and Raborn helped them in their other missile systems. Savvy was the CNO representative on all the committees and that sort of stuff. He was good, very good.

Q: I've read in various places that one of the Assistant Secretaries, Garry Norton, was very much interested in this subject. Was he of use to you?

Adm. B.: Yes, but again, this was just like a horse race - after a horse looks like he's going to win everybody's all for him. They all want a piece of the action. This doesn't detract from their support. It helps. He was helpful all along. When I say these things about people, it isn't unique to them, everybody does this. Nobody wants to support a losing game.

Q: Were you instrumental in getting Levering Smith into the picture?

Adm. B.: No.

Q: He had done some research himself back in the early fifties.

Burke - 36

Adm. B.: Yes. I think I gave Red a list of a lot of people, because I'd culled it quite well to help him, and Levering Smith, of course, would be on such a list. But, other than that, Red chose him. He chose the people.

Q: There was some emphasis, and rightly so as it turned out, on the public relations aspects of the program, in developing enthusiasm in industry and other places. Did you have something to do with this, with generating this emphasis?

Adm. B.: Maybe, but not very much. You've got to have support. I had an awful lot to do with impressing upon Red that he had to have support. For example, I gave him orders that he had my full authority to direct the bureaus, any bureau, if it ever came to that. I said, "You use that authority once, and you ruin the program, because you've got to get willing support. You can't get directed support. It's not good enough." This he did throughout. You have to have some public support. You have to have support all over to get anything done at all. So, to that extent, yes, but this was done by Red.

Authorization

The U.S. Naval Institute is hereby authorized to make available to individuals, libraries, and other repositories of its choosing the transcript (or portions thereof) of an oral history interview concerning the late Thomas S. Gates, Jr.'s involvement in the Polaris program. The interview was tape-recorded by Mr. Gates, in collaboration with Dr. John T. Mason, Jr. of the Naval Institute, on 3 October 1972.

Acting on behalf of the estate of the late Mr. Gates, the undersigned does hereby release and assign to the U.S. Naval Institute all right, title, restrictions, and interest in the interview. The tape recording of the interview shall be the sole property of the Naval Institute. The copyright in both the oral and transcribed versions shall also be the sole property of the Naval Institute.

Signed and sealed this 26th day of November, 1984.

Milicent B. Gates
(Mrs. Thomas S. Gates, Jr.)

DECLARATION OF TRUST

The undersigned does hereby appoint and designate as his (her) Trustee herein, the Secretary-Treasurer and Publisher of the United States Naval Institute to perform and discharge the following duties, powers, and privileges in connection with the possession and use of a certain taped interview between the undersigned and the Oral History Department of the United States Naval Institute.

1. Classification of Transcript.

( )a. If classified OPEN, the transcript(s) may be read or the recording(s) audited by the qualified personnel upon presentation of proper credentials, as determined by the Secretary-Treasurer of the U. S. Naval Institute.

(✓)b. If classified PERMISSION REQUIRED TO CITE OR QUOTE, the user will be required to obtain permission in writing from the interviewee prior to quoting or citing from either the transcript(s) or the recording(s).

( )c. If classified PERMISSION REQUIRED, permission must be obtained in writing from the interviewee before the transcribed interview(s) can be examined or the tape recording(s) audited.

( )d. If classified CLOSED, the transcribed interview(s) and the tape recording(s) will be sealed until a time specified by the interviewee. This may be until the death of the interviewee or for any specified number of years.

2. It is expressly understood that in giving this authorization, I am in no way precluded from placing such restrictions as I may desire upon use of the interview at any time during my lifetime, nor does this authorization in any way affect my rights to the copyright of my literary expressions that may be contained in the interview.

Witness my hand and seal this __8__ day of __May__ 19__73__.

_____

I hereby accept and consent to the foregoing Declaration of Trust and the powers therein conferred upon me as Trustee:

Interview with The Honorable Thomas S. Gates, Jr.

Place: His office in New York City

Date: Tuesday morning, 3 October 1972

Subject: Polaris Program

By: John T. Mason, Jr.

Q: Mr. Gates, I'm delighted that you will tell us something about the Polaris story as you saw it from the driver's seat in Washington.

Would you give me some of the background to the setting up of the Killian Committee to go through the whole subject and come up with recommendations to the President? The Committee report was presented, I believe, in early 1955.

Mr. G.: I can't give you any background on the setting up of the Killian Committee. That was set up by the President -

Q: It was, yes.

Mr. G.: - as a scientific advisory group, and their mission was to review all the various aspects of strategic defense, policies and programs, among other things. I had no hand in the creation of the Killian Committee. However, the Polaris idea was primarily developed within the Navy Department and, like other expensive and important weapon systems, came under the review of the scientific advisory group, whom the President relied on largely for technical advice in determining the priorities of these systems, from the point of view of time, capabilities, effectiveness, et cetera, and the point of view of funding the R and D.

My recollection is that the military side of the Navy Department was somewhat divided on the Polaris program initially. I think many of the people concerned questioned its technical capability. They questioned whether a missile of this size and importance could be placed on a submarine, as was planned, and at least some naval officers felt that the submarine would be about as big as a cruiser or a large destroyer, and we were going to have to invent a whole new kind of platform for this, which would be impractical.

Q: To some it seemed like an impossible undertaking, didn't it?

Mr. G.: Yes. An impossible dream really. The funny thing about it was that the enthusiasm - to oversimplify - for it came from the Bureau of Aeronautics, the aviators, although they emotionally were more involved than anybody else because this got into competition with the aircraft carrier system. But there were officers in the Bureau of Aeronautics that really were enthusiastic about the concept, whereas in the Bureau of Ordnance which had all the people really that had to work on the project and mesh the new designs of submarine and missile systems together there was pessimism about it, which was rather an anachronism because, as I say, the carrier was always under controversy as being a vulnerable system, and still is, yet it remains the highest priority requirement of the Navy.

Nonetheless, I found the aviators in the Bureau of Aeronautics agressively enthusiastic for trying Polaris, testing this project, and I found considerable reluctance within the Bureau of Ordnance, who had to do much of the job, under the Navy's organization, less enthusiastic.

Q: Were the aviators perhaps goaded on a bit by the knowledge that the Air Force was thinking about a missile?

Mr. G.: No. I think that was the chicken and the egg business. I think the Skybolt missile became an Air Force concept when the Polaris became a going development project. I think it was sort of the Air Force's answer to the Polaris program, rather than the other way round, although I'm not sure of that. I never really heard much about origins of the SKybolt missile. I got involved with Skybolt much later.

Q: At this point, you were deputy -

Mr. G.: That's when I heard and learned a lot about the Skybolt, when I was down at the Defense Department, but we're talking about the differences of opinion within the Navy family when I was in the Navy Department.

Q: When you were Under Secretary?

Mr. G.: In the beginning, yes. The result of this debate I think caused some problems in getting underway because, when called to support this project with initial funding, the Secretary of Defense got somewhat conflicting opinions from the Navy Department. I think it became rather clear that this was something that had to be done and could be done, but it could not be done under the existing organization of the Department of the Navy. Therefore we did something that had never been done before I don't believe in the Navy, and that was to establish a completely different form of organization for this project. We took it out of Bureau channels and set it up under a businesslike arrangement with a special project officer. Admiral Raborn was selected for that role, supported by the Bureaus, the Bureau of Ships for the submarines and the Bureau of Ordnance for the missile.

Q: When was this idea born?

Mr. G.: We, the Navy Secretariat, invented it, copying U. S. industry - applying it to government. It was born because the thing was on dead center and it was never going to get off dead center, and it was being questioned, I think, by some of the scientific advisory people from a technical point of view. It was obviously going to cost a lot of money and it was in competition with other systems, Army, Navy, and Air Force, and missile systems which were then coming into being in the Department of Defense, all of them very expensive and all of them very advanced, and all of them completely unproven technically. It was all a new world of war planning, strategic warfare, and of course that it was essential. Polaris seemed to be so vital and the odds were that it would work, so someone had to take a chance that it would work, and in order to see that it got proper support and monthly, if not daily, supervision, we set up this special office which, as I say, violated the traditional organization of the Navy Department, and set up in effect a board of directors that met formally, with minutes just the way you would do in business, to get the thing going and to follow it all the way through.

The board of directors consisted of myself and the Assistant Secretary of the Navy, first Mr. James Smith - Secretary Smith, later Secretary Garrison Norton, and the Vice Chief of Naval Operations, as I remember Admiral Duncan -

Q: Duncan?

Mr. G.: Wu Duncan, VCNO, and Admiral Raborn. There might have been and I think there was the chiefs of the Bureau of Ships and the Bureau of Ordnance, and maybe the head of the Office of Naval Research in the Navy Department. They were a board of directors that met weekly in the beginning and all reports were handed to them exactly the way you'd run it in business. It not only became important to get approval for this program and get the initial funding for it and to get technical support for it, but it became equally important during the course of the development of the systems because the system was certainly new. We learned a lot of things that we'd never learned before. We had to design not only a new submarine and a new missile and meld them together, but we had to learn new theories of navigation and we had to learn new theories of communication. I suspect that no one would have ever questioned the fact that the Navy didn't know more about navigation than anybody in the world, but this system created problems even for navigation. We found we didn't know everything about navigation.

Q: Certainly did.

Mr. G.: It also required a business system (PERT) in addition to the military system that was invented under the leadership of Admiral Raborn and his board of directors to mesh together something like 2,000 contractors, the principal contractor being the Lockheed Company who built a whole new plant in Sunnyvale, California, to coordinate and manage this project. I think that this new system, which subsequently was copied and is today being copied by a lot of people in large industry, was the first time it had ever been put together for a weapon system. I can talk more about that maybe a little later after we get involved with it.

Q: That's the projectizing?

Mr. G.: Yes. When we got all these ducks in a row in fairly good shape, we created a briefing position paper I guess you'd call it. I guess it was more like a book than a paper. It put together everything involved in this system, militarily, technically, moneywise, practically, personnel, policies, and training, in addition to all the rest of it. Then we had a question that we had to decide, go or no go. And I remember sending out a telegram to I think about forty chief executive officers of our largest American Industries, Lockheed, General Electric, Westinghouse, et cetera, and calling an emergency meeting of the chairmen of these companies. It was New Year's Eve 1957. It was a very important date. We urgently requested they meet in Washington and they all came, and we presented them for about two hours with this project in detail, then still on paper, and we sought their advice collectively.

Q: Had some of them had prior knowledge of some of the details of it, some of the problems?

Mr. G.: Yes, but only piecemeal. It was the first time they had the whole thing given to them from all angles. After a briefing of, I think, a whole morning --

Q: A lovely time!

Mr. G.: Well, there was a certain amount of urgency about it.

Q: Exactly. It underscores that fact.

Mr. G.: And they all came, which was very impressive for us because I think by then Lockheed was the sort of principal person, and they knew that. So they weren't competing for the leadership of the business. They weren't competing at all. We asked them to give the government their advice on whether this could be done, whether our cost figures were reasonably within the ball park, whether the technical boundaries were reasonably within the ball park, whether the timing was within the ball park - timing was very important, hence the urgency of the meeting.

After we briefed them in depth and detail and showed them the system we proposed to set up, to follow it daily with daily reports and daily photographs and daily charts of each component, we asked them for their frank judgment on whether this thing was doable or not. They agreed that it was doable.

Q: To a man?

Mr. G.: To a man. They agreed that it was going to be difficult, they agreed it was carving a new horizon, but they agreed that it was doable and spoke up and said, "Give us the ball and we'll take care of this thing for you if the United States needs it. If you need it, we'll do it." It was quite a dramatic performance.

Q: Indeed it was.

Mr. G.: And this came about as the result of pulling together this new organization and putting that new organization to work on it, having reviewed at the top level of the Navy through a board of directors, having it given highest priority attention by everyone concerned, and preparing this analysis in depth of all aspects of it.

Gates - 9

Then having it presented to the people who had to make the system work and were responsible for the principal components of it. Ultimately there were 2,200 sub-contractors involved, but in this particular meeting there were only about 40 or so involved - the top men of the top industries of the country.

Q: Who made the principal presentation at that meeting?

Mr. G.: It was made by a variety of people, as I recall. I presided and introduced the subject. Admiral Burke, the CNO, participated. Admiral Raborn made the principal presentation and pulled it together, but then he had on each aspect of it, the ship aspect, the missile aspect, the communication aspect, the electrical aspect, the technical side of it, intelligence, the best of qualified officers we had participated in the comprehensive review.

Q: Was Levering Smith in the picture at that time?

Mr. G.: Yes, he was. I think he was one of the people who also made a presentation at that meeting. Then when we got that go-ahead we unified in our position and went down and got approval. We got approval from the President and got going.

Q: May we lap back for a moment. You said this whole concept was developed because the proposed project was on dead center. Does this account for the delay in some action being taken by the President after he had received the Killian Report early in 1955?

He didn't actually make an official pronouncement until the 15th of September, shortly before his heart attack. This is the written record I'm quoting. And there's always been some question why the delay in the President taking some decision in the matter.

Mr. G.: I think the delay was that we hadn't pulled together a comprehensive analysis of all the facets of this thing, financial, technical, and so forth, in a unified and really in-depth proposal. We therefore couldn't get the approval of the Secretary of Defense to put this in the position of priority in which it should be put in his program. We had to do that first. I don't know whether that accounts for some of the delay on those particular dates or not, but it certainly accounted for delay. And it was proper delay, for that matter. This was a very important matter.

Q: Did you participate in briefing the President and supplying him with the necessary information on which to make the decision to go ahead?

Mr. G.: In the time sequence of Polaris I served as UnSecNav and SecNav both. The National Security Council always reviewed these high priority projects. Therefore the responsibility for the briefing of the President on this was really the responsibility of the Secretary of Defense. I didn't participate, as I recall, in personally briefing the President until later when we went to advanced missiles and we were in development and the question of how many missiles we'd have and the questions of the time factors and the financial factors involved were concerned. Then I did brief the President frequently, later on but not in the beginning.

Q: After he had given his go-ahead to it there was still further delay and, of course, this was complicated by his heart attack I presume, but then the Newberry Committee came into being. What is your recollection of that?

Mr. G.: Again, my recollection is somewhat hazy but I think the Newberry Committee was working for the Secretary of Defense, and the Secretary of Defense was faced with enormous pressures for priorities of big systems of missiles. A whole family of missiles was coming in after the Sputnik. We got pretty excited about this business, and, I said earlier, this was a completely new horizon. No one knew whether these missiles would work, even the land-based missiles, and our system was infinitely more complicated than the land-based missiles. We found we made many mistakes in the land-based-missile program, trying to develop and meld the hardware and the communications into the missiles per se. We couldn't make any Chinese copies of these things. They had to be done from new, and there was a tremendous urgency on the part of the United States to build and get going for the purposes of national security. We dug holes in the ground all over the country and we never knew whether these things would work or they wouldn't work.

Later on, when we got going on this program with even greater urgency, we had all the labor leaders and people into Washington along with the business people to try and remove any problems of jurisdictional strikes in various states. I remember conversations with George Meany, Walter Reuther, and others in this connection when I was in the Defense Department, and I think the Newberry Committee made the initial attempt to try and sort out where our efforts and emphasis should be because we couldn't do everything. And you certainly could never do everything in the numbers that the requirements, budgets of the military, which are always rather large. We not only couldn't afford to do it but we couldn't afford the manpower or the research to do it, to say nothing of the money.

I think because Newberry happened to be one of the first people appointed for applied engineering or something like that, the title of the Assistant Secretary of Defense, was a new organization which I think came in in 1956.

Q: Research and Engineering.

Mr. G.: Research and Engineering came later, I believe 1958. That was before we really had the power of the Director of Research which came later with Herb York when that office was created, which has been in existence ever since. It was a godsend to the Secretary of Defense when that office was created.

I think the Newberry was the initial attempt to look at the services. Don't forget the Army was heavily involved at this time, too, with Dr. von Braun and Huntsville, and the competition between the Army and Air Force and the Navy, bona fide competition, and the talent was rather dispersed between the three on who could do these things. This had to be organizationally sorted out, it had to be technically sorted out. I think the Newberry Committee was the sort of listening post for the Secretary of Defense to see how much of this could be done and how real it was in a real world which we all agreed, including the Secretary of Defense and the President, required the highest degree of urgency.

Q: When the Secretary of Defense finally gave the green light to the Navy again, it was primarily as I remember the written record, to go ahead and cooperate with the Army on Jupiter in the thought that perhaps Jupiter could be adapted.

Mr. G.: Correct.

Q: Yet the Navy at the time were thinking of their own project, were they not?

Mr. G.: Yes, because I don't think the Navy had any confidence, and I think correctly so, that the Jupiter thrust requirements and size requirements could ever be adapted to a submarine system. People in this new world tended to oversimplify the problem in terms of, "Well, one missile versus another missile and maybe we could have a common missile," or something like that. And put it to sea as well as on land. Maybe we could have, I don't know, but it didn't seem very practical to us. It seemed to us that it was quite a different game.

Q: A solid-fuel propellant was one of the chief factors?

Mr. G.: That's correct. The main factor. If that had not proven out there would never have been a Polaris system. The small warhead made it possible.

Q: Did you have something to do with the development of that in the scientific world?

Mr. G.: Only listen! Basically that was under the AEC and the Pacific test programs.

Q: I mean in goading them to do something about it.

Mr. G.: Oh yes, certainly. It was an approved military requirement

Q: I believe the Secretary of Defense also ordered that if the Navy wanted to go ahead and develop something of their own, they had to finance it out of their existing budget. How did the Navy react to this?

Mr. G.: That's a sort of historic game in the Department of Defense which I played along with every other Secretary of Defense. If you want it you've got to pay for it. They didn't react well to it, but that is always a question of a little and both. I mean, obviously, if the Navy or the Air Force or the Army wanted to develop any very expensive weapon system of this character they had to cut something else out to some extent. You couldn't have everything. The country could not afford everything in terms of either money or manpower. You can't have three new aircraft carriers and forty submarines. You've got to pick and choose, and it's always difficult to do because a case can be made for everyone's requirements. We always believed there could be no Defense unless there was a sound American economy. So balance of judgments was vital.

Q: That's where your problems within the family come in !

Mr. G.: That's a management problem for the Secretary of Defense, and it's a tough one. The Army, of course has a very difficult time with this because a very large proportion of their budget goes to support people. They have the biggest numbers of people The maintenance and operations expenses of the Army are very high, and there's very little they can cut out of their budget to carry on an enormous weapons development unless they cut people out.

So I would say that that problem's historic, it's always been there, it's probably there right now today, I'm sure it is, and subsequent Secretaries of Defense have just had to pick and choose. It's a little of both. It's a little out of the Defense budget, it's a little out of the Navy budget, it's a little out of the things that will be approved by the President's budget. But it isn't all based on money always. It's also based on time and technical priorities. And then, how many numbers do you require? I mean, there used to be in the later days when I was involved with the Defense Department a continuous requirement for Minuteman missiles. It was about four times as much as anybody ever thought we could afford or need, but it stayed in there all the years I was there. I'm sure the Navy would rather have had 150 submarines than the 40 they finally got approved. So there's a little give and take all along the line from the standpoint of reality.

Q: Did you have any particular problems within the Navy Department once you began to juggle things around in order to get adequate funds to finance Polaris?

Mr. G.: Yes. One always has problems --

Q: Can you cite any of them?

Mr. G.: Well, there were probably many of them in a small way because this kind of an exercise whittles down to whether we can afford or need as urgently as something else, a drydock at Newport News, which is very expensive, maybe $100 million or something like that, or whether we need another aircraft carrier which is a more important decision or whether we can modernize our destroyers and set up a greater Fleet Air Defense System, which in total is probably the most expensive system the Navy ever developed. It is a complex of missiles, aircraft, destroyers, and submarines, how much of that, and everybody who had to cut back on something felt they had a good case, if they had the right numbers to do the right job with. And, looking at it from a parochial point of view, they did, but it had to be weighed against the priority of something else.

Sure, there's always a problem about this because the initial program of the CHief of Naval Operations or the Chief of Staff of the other services is always internally, in those departments, based on higher requirements than the Secretaries of those departments will ever approve, forgetting about what the Secretary of Defense has to do. It has to fit the approved JSOP basic policy and the approved mobilization base requirements over all. There are a great many decisions in this process made by the service Secretary before it ever gets to the Secretary of Defense. You know, continuous meetings and reviews which is a process daily almost twelve months a year.

Yes, I think there were always difficulties about this, but it never works out that you have to absorb it all. Somebody else absorbs pieces of it, and even then you increase the Defense Budget. You absorb some of the problem and the Secretary of Defense sees that the other services absorb some of the problem, and you absorb some of their problems. It crosses lines and that's what the Director of Research and Engineering guides the Secretary of Defense on. Later on, when he became important in this respect and spoke with great authority and had his own scientific advisors to help him, working in coordination with the President's Scientific Advisory Board.

Q: Would you talk, Sir, about the system of awarding contracts, which was outside of the prescribed procedure, for Polaris?

Mr. G.: I don't really recall how we happened to select the Lockheed Company. I'm sure they were selected under some method of competitive appraisal of ability to perform as the principal contractor, and I'm sure that this was agreed to within the Department of the Navy without any question as to their being the people who could best do the job. Then the question of the components was left to Lockheed as manager and the Special Projects office who could overrule the Bureau in terms of who did this work. The Bureaus made their recommendations, you know, who was going to build some of the submarines, which is done on a competitive basis, who was going to do something else in terms of all these contractors, guided by Lockheed and guided by judgments within the Navy Department. There was not much controversy about who was the best to do the job.

Q: It was more direct than the normal procedure?

Mr. G.: Much more direct because it was centralized. It was run just like a business, and every aspect of it was reported formally to this so-called board of directors, of which Raborn was the executive who worked for this board of directors. He didn't work for the Chief of Naval Operations really the way he normally would have, and he didn't work exactly, precisely, for the Secretary the way he normally would have, although technically he did. He worked for this board of directors that represented both the military and the civilian show.

Q: In a legal sense, the Secretary had delegated some of his authority to Raborn, had he not?

Mr. G.: No. Only if he wanted to. He could have done anything he wanted. He is the Chief Executive Officer. We preferred to function in a partnership director form of management, rather than by arbitrarily assuming that we knew all the answers. In this new world that we were living in, we all learned a lot as we went along by this procedure.

Q: You had to give a terrific amount of time, did you not?

Mr. G.: An enormous amount of time. More time than anybody had spent on anything before. Yes.

Q: Admiral Burke said that, as a system it worked in his opinion, because it was the only one underway at that time. If there had been two or three special projects underway, he didn't think that it would have succeeded.

Mr. G.: I agree. And that was something that worried me a great deal, and it was used against me and the civilian secretariat to set this office up. They said we're going to violate the Navy organization and everything is going to become a special project because the costs and technical capabilities of these things — the technical requirements of these things are so vast now that there's a very good case that even a Fleet Air Defense certainly is a special project. It involves three kinds of ships and all kinds of communications and all kinds of weapons. Why not have a special project for that? And there was a very strong, I think, traditional type of opposition to the creation of this office.

Q: From whom primarily? From the Congress?

Mr. G.: No, from the naval officers.

Q: Did the Congress offer any objections to a special project —?

Mr. G.: I don't think we bothered to consult them about it in the beginning, and afterwards I think they began to live with it all right and liked it. It would be perfectly characteristic if some people who were traditionalists in the form of organization perfection would talk to the Congress in their testimony about their preference would have been to have left it with the Bureau of ships and the Bureau of Ordnance, coordinated in the normal fashion with the CNO and the Secretary and not have a Special Projects office. It would have been perfectly normal to have that judgment. It was the judgment of a good many people. This was not exactly a popular idea to start with.

Q: Wll, it's the kind of objection which the Congress raised, which Carl Vinson himself raised, when you attempted a reorganization in 1958. The Congress was abdicating its traditional right to appropriate for specific things, and they were doing the same thing interms of Polaris, weren't they?

Mr. G.: Carl Vinson was a great man, one of the best ever in the Congress, but this all went in the Navy budget. One of the best committees in the Congress is the Appropriations Committee of the House, and they got every detail all along. George Mahon and Gerry Ford and their colleagues are very experienced people and they knew all the whole story in depth. The Armed Services Committee did, too, of course. I never recall any problem with the Congress in regard to the Polaris system. As a matter of fact, I think maybe the problem with the Congress with regard to the Polaris system, when this thing started to catch hold it was so imaginative, maybe the problem with the Congress was overenthusiasm. We were always afraid that we might, you know, have some failures and something wouldn't work. In a very fortunate way, Polaris became the good boy of all the missile systems of the country. Not only a good boy in concept, but a good boy in development. We had very few mistakes, very few failures of tests en route. Every other system, even simpler airplane weapon systems, had a lot of failures. We had very good luck, and let's call it some good management, too, in terms of everybody connected with the Polaris system, and it was really the best-behaved boy, as it was, of course, the most imaginative one. So we had no trouble with the Congress, except they wanted to give us all the money in the world for it!

Q: Overly generous!

Gates - 22

Mr. G.: Yes. In fact, they wanted to push, push, push. Thus they were both helpful and right.

Q: Would you talk about the safeguards you wrote, so to speak, into the planning? The possible cut-off dates.

Mr. G.: Yes. There was an accountability system established with some initials - the PREP system. This system was devised to manage this project, and it was to manage it so that we were aware all the time with requirements from everybody concerned in even a minor piece of equipment in regard to this system, furnishing weekly reports which were put on charts and photographed in a war room. A war room was created for the management of this system. We knew exactly where everything was in the question of time, so that we could then gauge whether something was going to delay a piece of equipment or a communications something or other, delay the total results, or delay some tests, or delay the program and it would therefore be even more expensive, and maybe even show some bugs up that might mean we had to call the whole thing off because we had to invent a lot of this technology —

Q: As it was manufactured?

Mr. G.: As it was manufactured. The beauty of this system was that even the most humble - I'm not sure it wasn't even the paint on the submarine, everything was charted weekly and we knew exactly where everybody stood. And Raborn could sit on top of that thing with his staff, and his board of directors were sitting on top of it. He'd report to us. We'd go to that room and look. "Here's where we stand on this," and "Look at this fellow, he's behind." Then we'd put the heat on him and see whether he needed help or whether we needed a new research game going or a new technical piece of advice from somebody else, or he's just a sloppy worker. We could put the pressure on the spots that would keep the whole thing synchronized.

Q: Arleigh Burke said there were two or three occasions, as he recalled it, when it looked as though you were going to arrive at a cut-off time. Do you remember those? Do you remember anything about them?

Mr. G.: You mean stop it?

Q: Yes.

Mr. G.: No, I don't remember we ever got quite that close to a cut-off time. I remember we were concerned about certain of these pieces going together and we held our breaths when certain of these tests were conducted, and all of us made trips to Sunnyvale, California, where this was pulled together by Lockheed. They were the managers of the whole thing. And we had frequent breath-holding exercises. Very frankly, none of us were as optimistic that things would go quite as well as they did. I mean we expected more trouble than we encountered. We were, I guess, blessed!

Q: Was the AEC having any problem with the development of the warhead? And were you cognizant of that, or were they ahead of schedule in what they were doing?

Mr. G.: The solid-propellant was the big problem. With that warhead we thought we had the answer. They'd done it before, but I don't recall that they had any great problem that delayed anything, after they accomplished the major breakthrough.

This system has got to be so precise in knowing exactly where the missile was launched from from the point of view of navigation because your targeting system, which is a whole other subject which we got into later, about how we handled that, had to be so precise that we had to do a lot of new work, and we wanted to do it in the framework of the highest priority and the highest urgency. And the Air Force, with no reflection on the Air Force at all, tried to do the same thing with their land-based missiles and ran into great difficulty and great delay on matching the plumbing with the missile We thought our system was more complex than that, and I think it was when you consider all the various aspects of command and control related to Polaris.

I just don't really know why we were quite as fortunate as we were, but it happened to be just the right idea at the right time and it happened to work. As I say, the management was unique and different, nothing was ever managed before that way, and it's a great credit to Admiral Raborn and the people that served under him that this came about.

Q: Would you talk a little about the development of this feeling of urgency? This was, of course, before Sputnik when the whole thing got underway.

Mr. G.: Well, every system got quite a lift after Sputnik.

Q: Oh, yes, indeed. Lots of things happened after Sputnik, but before there was still a sense of urgency. How was this generated within the government or the country? Were the people cognizant of the urgency?

Mr. G.: I think that the development of nuclear weapons, the development of technology, the development of everything came so rapidly that we could see whole new requirements in light of what was happening. I went there in 1953, and, as I think I told you in another interview, there wasn't an airplane that could beat the speed of sound. There was not a missile in existence, and there were all kinds of other things that weren't in existence in terms of modern communications. The whole technical revolution came about and we were perfectly aware that the Russians were working on this, and yet we had to maintain a lot of defense in terms of traditional numbers of people and equipment. So there was always the question of how much money you spent or how much time you spent on new technologies in the new world of possibilities. People could think up the most fascinating things in the world. And it all happened in a very, very tight time span. I'd say in two or three years. That doesn't mean that work hadn't been going on on these things for ten years before, because of course they were. But it all kind of came about all at once, and you began to question, you know, the real strategic importance of some of the major things we owned in our forces. We began to question the capability of our guns, the capability of our ships, the capability of our communications, everything. And the Soviet threat was building up. In NATO and in conversation, they were developing their technologies and their systems. Mr. K. was aggressive and talking. We were in a new ball game and it came very fast.

Q: It was almost an about-face, however, from what the President was trying to develop. You remember, the Spirit of Geneva, the atoms for peace, and the whole emphasis in this direction. And suddenly there was this great sense of urgency.

Mr. G.: Well, it was always, I think, important to try and negotiate arms limitations, which were signed yesterday in Washington and started way back then. It's always important to try to make progress with treaties and atoms-for-peace projects. Sure, President Eisenhower worked about as hard as anybody ever did for peace, but that didn't mean that you could neglect your strategic capabilities. As a matter of fact, there was every reason not to neglect them at that time because our relations were greatly more strained. We were firm believers in leading from strength.

Q: Would you say something, Sir, about the remarkable spirit of team work which was engendered by this project in industry, the man on the lathe, that sort of thing, the whole sense of cooperation? How was this inspired? Did the board of directors have anything to do with it?

Mr. G.: I think we convinced ourselves and we convinced our superiors and industry and the public and the Congress that the country required this system, and it was bona fide. There wasn't any credibility gap of any kind. It was a bona fide requirement and it was a challenge and it had very good leadership - good management and good leadership. That slopped over down to the lowest man. There was continuous communication, as I told you, in the war room, but also in personal visits at all levels. I don't know how many times I went to Sunnyvale myself, where this was being pulled together from a management point of view, other than what Raborn was managing in a reporting sense and keeping on top of in Washington. The pieces of this were also managed by Lockheed at Sunnyvale, and very obviously with dedicated, skilled workers. In the first place, the whole plant was built to do this project. People were hired for this job. There was nothing at Sunnyvale but a field. I don't know how many thousands of men they ended up with in that place, but a great many.

It was well done by Lockheed, it was well done by Raborn, and the country said we needed the system and we're going to make it work.

Gates - 28

Q: Were you involved in the public relations aspect of it, as by that time you were Secretary of the Navy?

Mr. G.: Continuously.

Q: Making speeches?

Mr. G.: Continuously. They were constant, and public relations aspects with our allies, and dealing with our NATO friends as well.

Q: Tell me something about that.

Mr. G.: The British, of course, wanted to develop this system, and the French wanted to develop the system. Later on, when I was in the Defense Department, there was an idea advanced by the Secreatry of State at a NATO meeting that we have a multilaterial force of Polaris submarines, manned by multinational crews.

Q: Hadn't we learned with the CLAUDE V. RICKETTS?

Mr. G.: About the problems involved? Well, it looked, on paper, like a good idea and we were trying to walk that line, that difficult line, between nationalism on the part of the French and ambitions on the part of the British, their respective capabilities, and also be good allies in NATO. Again, it was a priority question of who could do the most best, who could make the contribution in their own style in the best fashion. This business of defense is always a matter of difficult judgment.

Q: How up to date did you keep our principal allies as this project developed?

Mr. G.: Almost completely.

Q: This is the British and the French?

Mr. G.: Principally. Of course, we had a closer relationship on atomic knowledge with the British, which is one thing President de Gaulle didn't like very much. As a matter of fact it was one reason — the reason, I guess — that he went to his force de frappe. He didn't like our closer arrangements with the British. But the British were continously informed.

Q: Did they through their scientific endeavor contribute anything to the development of Polaris?

Mr. G.: I don't think so. I say that sort of cautiously because the British have contributed so very much particularly to naval systems, radar and canted decks, steam catapults, and all kinds of innovations. They always have fascinated me in aviation and the advanced part of military life, how much the British radar, to begin with — they invented ...

Q: Watson-Watt, yes.

Gates - 30

Mr. G.: And I think it has always fascinated me to see how much the British could contribute and how they never are really capable of developing the systems themselves but they could invent it, and then someone else has to put it all together.

Q: A lack of lesser industrial set-up, I suppose.

Mr. G.: Yes, I suppose so, and resources.

Q: As the program went along, do you want to talk about the latter phases of it?

Mr. G.: The most important latter phase was probably the summer of 1960 when we decided to increase the defense budget and the defense capabilities, and thought we had good reason to do so because of the threat facing us. Then there was the question of what the second phase of the Polaris would be, and there was some difference of opinion on that. I was then Secretary of Defense and Bill Franke was Secretary of the Navy and I think the judgment had to be made there as to whether we were going to increase the Polaris program and the question was how. One way to increase it was to increase the number of approved systems, jump up the numbers of submarines approved and missiles to go with them. The other was to go immediately all-out into a longer-range missile then only on a drawing board. Secretary Franke and I together decided to go for the longer-range missile - to complete the program, as planned, and accelerate it, if possible, but not to increase the authorized strength and numbers of Polaris submarines and missiles, but to take that additional effort and put into a new longer-range missile.

That went through its process until now, today, and the Navy is on the third missile, called I believe the Trident, which is even better than the second and certainly infinitely better than the first.

Q: Success breeds success, I guess.

Mr. G.: Yes, but the Trident is going to be enormously expensive, according to the present Chief of Naval Operations, whom I happened to meet with last week, and probably again a very diffucult proposal. You see, when you took this whole missile business up, from the Secretary of Defense's point of view, you were spending in superficially stated round numbers a couple of billion dollars a year on each of these things. First, Jupiter, Thor, and then Atlas, then Minuteman, then Polaris, then testing, and whether you should go into production or you shouldn't go into production, and involving building enormous complexes to test, like at Vandenberg Air Force Base in California, and firing missiles to Kwajalein to see whether we could intercept them or not, and testing the problem of decoys and multiple warheads, the MIRV systems, which were then coming along. This was an expensive effort, not only in terms of money but in terms of manpower and scientific availability. We were employing every scientist there was in the country. Till the space people came along we had them all! I don't know how many of them were out at Kwajalein. That was an Air Force system, but Polaris was in competition with others. We don't need all of them and we don't need all the numbers that some people would like to have. We had to make the judgments that went with them and then we had to develop the strategic targeting problem that went with them and the command and control problems that went with them.

All these were great factors of judgment, and not just a once-a-year review. It was continuously following progress, continously working with all phases of the thing to see where we were slipping, which was better, which looked better, which would do the better job, and in light of enemy developments as well.

Q: You say that as you got along into that stage of things you were constantly advising the President. What was his reaction to the whole development? How did he feel about it?

Mr. G.: Well, he was of course a military man, number one, so he understood the language completely. He was personally extremely interested. We were in competition on two or three different airplane systems at the same time, as well as these missile systems. We had the B-59 airplane, the B-70, then a requirement of the Defense Department. It was under review again by the Scientific Advisory Board and at that time the Director of Research and Engineering, and the President wanted to be and was fully informed on each of these systems, their progress, their cost, their requirements, and their capabilities. Everybody had their share of telling the President what was good or what was bad about this whole thing, including the Scientific Advisory groups because there were technical questions of great importance involved with each one of these things.

So the President was completely briefed and particularly briefed on the command and control and planning aspects.

Q: I would think it was fortunate we had a president at that time, as Polaris developed, who could understand the military aspect?

Mr. G.: It was helpful. Well, I think we were fortunate in President Eisenhower in a great many ways. That was one way. Another way was he was not really involved in the political aspects of it. He wasn't influenced by political difficulties which most presidents are not influenced by but it takes more time to handle them, and he worried about handling them. I'm not talking from a partisan point of view. I mean a political president has to spend more attention on such things than D. D. E. was willing to do. That wasn't very good for the Republican Party, but it was very good for the U. S. and for us in Defense!

Q: Would you clarify one minor point — well, not so minor, but a point which is not clear in my mind, and that is the determination on forty submarines? How was this arrived at?

Mr. G.: I really don't know precisely, but I'm sure it was arrived at two ways. The normal way of how long on station and how many on station, which is the rotation problem of ships, the same as to keep one carrier on station you need three carriers, one in port, one on route, and one on station. The same principle applies to a submarine, and this was a difficult assignment for the crews of these ships. It was tough duty on a Polaris submarine. We needed new skills and the men were deployed for long periods. So we had personnel problems that contributed to the question, which was how many on station. It was also related to the contribution they were going to make to the total targeting problem. How many did you need for deterrent and how would they fit in with the contributions made by the Department of Defense as a whole? How many missiles should be delivered, where, and in order to do that, how many ships should you have on station? How long could they stay there? And this added up to a reasonable contribution and seemed to fall into the forty ship level.

Q: In connection with that subject, did you have any role in the preliminaries to the establishment of the base at Rota and the one in Scotland?

Mr. G.: Yes. The base at Rota came about because we were in effect no longer welcome in Port Lyautey, which was an important naval base of long standing, and we had to search elsewhere for a base and the Air Force had an agreement with the Spanish government to build Spanish bases and a pipeline to go with them and this happened to come in through Rota and go on up to supply the Air Force bases in Spain which were agreed to or under construction at that particular time under an arrangement with the Spanish government.

When the Navy had to phase out of Port Lyautey we needed a base somewhere at that end of the Mediterranean, and Rota looked like the best location to our experts. I never was quite sure why it was because it seemed to me to be very unprotected.

Q: Did you go and inspect there?

Mr. G.: Oh, yes.

Q: John Lodge had a role in that, did he not?

Mr. G.: John was our Ambassador there. We spent a lot of money and we built a hell of a fine naval base at Rota. It came about from a bona fide requirement. We couldn't keep Port Lyautey and we had to go some place, and we had cooperative arrangements already in hand with the Spaniards in terms of the Air Force. So this seemed to fit into the total Defense complex reasonably easily politically and seemed to be satisfactory militarily.

Q: What about the Scottish base?

Mr. G.: The Scottish base was not a base, was it? It was mostly home-porting.

Q: Home-porting, yes.

Mr. G.: Yes. That's again a personnel problem, re-fueling, and re-furnishing problem, and geographically Scotland was an ideal place for that. It seemed to fit into the general area of distribution of the submarines rather well, the British were our allies and enthusiastic about what we were doing. At that time, they were fussing with the Skybolt missile which became a political controversy in England greater than it ever did in America. And it looked like a natural home-port type of arrangement. We did run into, as we did in Japan and elsewhere on occasion, the question of the safety and security of nuclear submarines. It had nothing really to do with the Polaris. It had to do with the nuclear submarines.

Q: You mean when it went into a port?

Mr. G.: Yes. Public opinion developed in certain areas, including Scotland, rather dramatically that they didn't want those ships in their port from a public relations point of view.

Q: They felt they might be a focal point for an attack from the enemy?

Mr. G.: Yes, or they thought there might be an accident — an accident that would cause a leak and cause contamination, and the well-meaning, peace-loving advocates -- anti-military advocates, I guess "doves" may be a good word, were concerned and they stirred up public relations and newspaper opposition.

Q: It became a matter of education, then?

Mr. G.: A matter of education. Sometimes it's very difficult to educate over a short haul!

Q: That leads me to another question. You spoke about the vast army of scientists who were engaged in the development of the Polaris. At that point in time, anti-military attitude hadn't permeated their ranks?

Mr. G.: Yes, but to a lesser extent. We had von Neumanns and we had Killians, Herb York, Oscar Morganestern, and we had commissions and we had George Kistiakowsky, among others. And we had the beginnings of the whole system of scientific advisory boards. The Navy had that even before that. The Navy had scientific advisory committees in World War II under Forrestal, and the Office of Naval Research was created under Forrestal. They had scientific advisors.

We had coordination. I was told once but I've never checked this that the Navy were responsible for most of the research done in the United States up until shortly before this period we're talking about, after World War II. The Navy financed college research nationally through the Office of Naval Research.

Q: I think you're right.

Mr. G.: And I think that was one of the reasons the Office of Naval Research was created. It was not just to serve the Navy but to serve the nation in mobilizing some government research. My friend Luis de Flores had a hand in advising Forrestal to set that up. One of the great things that they did there was not really to serve themselves but to serve the country.

This all existed, but it didn't exist on the scale or in the numbers that were required to invent new systems.

Q: And it wasn't concentrated on that?

Mr. G.: No.

Q: You were talking off tape about the fact that it was such a widespread effort and that many people deserve credit.

Mr. G.: Yes, the credit belongs all along the line. It belongs to American industry and its workers, it belongs to the naval officers, it belongs to the civilians and the scientists. It was a gigantic effort to which many people made very important contributions. Admiral Raborn headed the project and of course deserves much credit for it because he made it be pulled together and made it fit. But we all had a hand in it and it was a national program of the highest possible priority and importance. So its success must be shared by everyone who contributed toward it.

Q: A concluding question, Sir. In the light of what has transpired since then, do you think a project of this proportion and nature could be accomplished today?

Mr. G.: I think the Polaris project convinced me that the United States can do anything it wants to do, provided we're willing to mobilize the effort and the support that goes with it. We put men on the moon and that was maybe even more remarkable than the Polaris. Probably was more remarkable than Polaris. It was, not "probably," it was more remarkable, and I learned in this period of great change that research never plateaued. It kept on going. And technology kept on going. I thought after we sort of topped out about 1960 or 1965 or sometime in there we would replace everything we owned in the Defense Department and up-date it and have a period of maybe thirty or forty years where we wouldn't have to worry about technology continuing to increase because the change had been so very vast that it would take us a while to digest it, but that never happened.

Once upon a time that same Luis de Flores I mentioned before, who is now dead, came in to see me when I was secretary of Defense and said, "I think you're wasting your time with all these systems you're creating here. Why don't you learn how to control the weather? There's no problem about controlling the weather. All you've got to do is put your mind to it." And I think he's probably right.

Q: I'm glad that you ended on that note of optimism. I hoped you would. Thank you very much.

DECLARATION OF TRUST

The undersigned does hereby appoint and designate as his (her) Trustee herein, the Secretary-Treasurer and Publisher of the United States Naval Institute to perform and discharge the following duties, powers, and privileges in connection with the possession and use of a certain taped interview between the undersigned and the Oral History Department of the United States Naval Institute.

1. Classification of Transcript.

    ( )a. If classified OPEN, the transcript(s) may be read or the recording(s) audited by the qualified personnel upon presentation of proper credentials, as determined by the Secretary-Treasurer of the U. S. Naval Institute.

    ( )b. If classified PERMISSION REQUIRED TO CITE OR QUOTE, the user will be required to obtain permission in writing from the interviewee prior to quoting or citing from either the transcript(s) or the recording(s).

    ( )c. If classified PERMISSION REQUIRED, permission must be obtained in writing from the interviewee before the transcribed interview(s) can be examined or the tape recording(s) audited.

    ( )d. If classified CLOSED, the transcribed interview(s) and the tape recording(s) will be sealed until a time specified by the interviewee. This may be until the death of the interviewee or for any specified number of years.

    It is expressly understood that in giving this authorization, I am in no way precluded from placing such restrictions as I may desire upon use of the interview at any time during my lifetime, nor does this authorization in any way affect my rights to the copyright of my literary expressions that may be contained in the interview.

Witness my hand and seal this 20th day of March 1979

_____

I hereby accept and consent to the foregoing Declaration of Trust and the powers therein conferred upon me as Trustee:

_____

Interview with Mr. Carleton Shugg

        Mystic, Connecticut

Place of interview: New York City

Date: Friday morning, 16 November 1973

Subject: The Polaris Project

By: John T. Mason, Jr.

Q: Mr. Shugg, I'm delighted to meet you in the flesh at last. I've heard a lot about you from Jimmy Fife and others, and I know that you're a very important part of this whole Polaris project.

    I wonder if you'd begin this interview by telling me a little about your own background?

Mr. S.: Well, my background is that of a rolling stone, perhaps! I graduated from the Naval Academy in 1920, went to sea for a year, became chief engineer of a destroyer, and then came back for three years of postgraduate work under the Navy's auspices.

Q: In ordnance?

Mr. S.: In naval construction, and the last two years of that were spent at MIT where, aside from the general studies, we had to pick a specific design of combat ship to work on for those two years. I picked submarines and therefore when I'd finished at Tech I went to practically the only government submarine yard, which was at Portsmouth, New Hampshire. I worked there through a wonderful period of development. The Navy was designing and building larger submarines, the V class; in addition to major alterations on different classes of WW II boats. There was the salvage and repair of several sunken or wrecked submarines, such as the S-4, and I ended up by being the Bureau of Construction and Repair technical officer in connection with the safety and salvage studies that were made after the lessons of the S-4, including the escape lung and the rescue bell.

That brought me up to a very dull period in the Navy, with the limitation of armaments treaty in force, and a classmate persuaded me to join him in electronics manufacturing. So I resigned my commission at the end of 1929.

Q: At that moment, it didn't look like much of a future, did it, in the Navy?

Mr. S.: No, it looked as if it would be fifteen years before I got another half-stripe, but I hadn't foreseen Franklin D. Roosevelt and I went with this classmate for ten years, making electronic parts.

Q: Where was this?

Mr. S.: That is now - and it was then too - Sprague Electric Company. By the end of the 1930s, that's ten years and brings it up to 1940, I was still in the Naval Reserve as a naval constructor, inactive, and there was enough indication of excitement in my original game, shipbuilding so the Chief of the Bureau, after being asked, advised me to go to Cramp Shipbuilding Company and take part in the reopening of that mothballed ship yard.

I spent three years there, when a change at the top and the realization that the interests financing Cramp were not serious about continuing the yard after the war, led to my departure from there and my going to Todd Shipyards where I spent the war at two ship yards in Hoboken and in Brooklyn.

Q: What did Todd turn out primarily?

Mr. S.: Todd was primarily a repair and conversion outfit. At the end of the war I had charge of these two yards with a total of about 35,000 men and 14 dry docks. This was a madhouse job of handling ships anywhere in the port of New York, at piers in the North River, the East River, down the Bay, twenty-four hours a day seven days a week. We handled everything from tugs and floats to the biggest liners and semi-combat ships, and naval auxiliary ships.

After the war, of course, that activity just took a nose

dive and it became a very routine operation, so I looked around for something new and went with the Atomic Energy Commission at its outset of civilian control, first as manager of the Hanford operations, that's the platonium-manufacturing plant, then back to Washington as Deputy General Manager.

Q: What did you know about atomic energy at that point? What led you in that direction?

Mr. S.: The fact that I knew nothing about it, and it was therefore a very exciting proposition. It was in the first days of civilian control of atomic energy and it was a case of snapping out of the lethargy that pervaded the project after the cessation of hostilities. There was a tremendous expansion, and I wouldn't have missed it for anything.

Well, when I came back to Washington as Deputy General Manager I was also acting director of the Division of Reactor Development, which had been recently established but had no Director. That brought me, as having had some submarine experience and also by that time being able to at least speak some of the language of atomic energy, into pretty direct contact with the proposal to build a nuclear-propelled submarine. After I had been in Washington two and a half years David Lilienthal, the Chairman, resigned. the General Manager resigned too, and as I was really a part of their team, I left also. The new regime needed their own man and I went on to Electric

Boat to see the Nautilus project at least to completion.

I did see the Nautilus project through but before it was finished there were several other equally interesting projects started and under way, so that before I knew it, the end of ten years was approaching and I would ordinarily have left EB because it was my lifetime conviction that a production man shouldn't be in the same spot longer than ten years - and this goes for any production game. A man shoots his wad in any one situation, I think, in under ten years and after that he doesn't justify himself.

Q: Especially a man with such driving energy as you have!

Mr. S.: Wittingly or unwittingly, it's time to move on. But about the time I was beginning to feel that way the Polaris project came along and that was too hot and too fascinating to miss so I stayed on to see that well under way.

Q: Did you get involved with that immediately in 1955, when Raborn came to Washington?

Mr. S.: Yes, we were in touch with it from the beginning and when it came to building the submarines I was called to Washington and the first Polaris submarines were allotted, as it were, between what the Bureau considered the best five yards and we at EB got two out of the five. As a matter of fact, it was originally contemplated that we'd get three out of five, but they were all hot as to their timetable. We got the first two for delivery - the first two to be delivered were assigned to us, and the other yards were assigned one apiece of the last three.

Q: When was this decision actually made to assign two of them to you? After Sputnik?

Mr. S.: I'm sorry to say I've forgotten the exact years now. It may have been December 1957, does that sound right to you?

Q: Yes, that was the time of Sputnik.

Mr. S.: The whole thing was the experience of a lifetime because I remember that I went down to this Bureau meeting just before Christmas and it was simply the Chief's word there that we would receive a contract for the first two.

Q: Mumma was Chief?

Mr. S.: Yes, Al Mumma was Chief. I went back and put my gang to work on it. The important thing was to get steel on order before the end of the month because the rolling mills were scheduled by the month and we didn't want to miss thirty days. My man responsible came over to my house on Christmas Day with all of the mill orders for steel, which were based on an estimate of what we would need, and we got the steel on order before ever seeing a piece of paper. And we made other heavy commitments, and that was the way the relationship was between

EB and the Bureau. You asked me to cover that at one time.

Q: Merely an act of faith!

Mr. S.: Well, it's the way business should be done more often. I mean we each knew the other. I can expand on that.

Q: It's not the way government business is done ordinarily?

Mr. S.: No, because now we're in an age of everybody cirticizing everybody else and Monday morning quarterbacking finds something that could have been done better or that wasn't exactly right. When I went to Hanford, I was given a definite timetable there to meet in as much under five years as possible, a certain production figure, and it was made under twenty-four months. In order to do that, you just have to take some chances. The legal counsel there was very understanding. I had a set-to with him at the outset and I told him I expected to be investigated, I expected to be tried, if you will, and that I wasn't trying to keep out of jail but his job was to adivse which of several possible alteratives would get me the shortest sentence! From then on, we rolled.

Now, you asked about winding up my own experience.

In 1962 the topside of General Dynamics Corporation was turned over and the new President wanted me to come to the New York headquarters office. I also was a vice president of the Corporation. So I left Electric Boat after twelve years instead of ten and went to the coporate headquarters in New York, and stayed there until my retirement at the age of 65 in 1964. I continued on as a consultant for about three years, and finally terminated all relationships with General Dynamics at the end of 1967.

Q: A fabulous and productive career!

Mr. S.: After a half year of loafing, I went into another game I didn't know anything about, which was the bond business. I still work part time at that. You can see why I said "rolling stone."

Q: Well, let's go back now to the Polaris itself. Tell me some of the details of the construction of the submarine under the aegis of BuShips.

Mr. S.: As you know, the timetable on the first deployment of the first Polaris submarines was extremely tight. We were asked to get the George Washington out in two years and, although the Bureau's "contract designs", those are the over-all plans, had been under way for some time, the detailed design had not started when I went to Washington that December. We were asked to do the detailed design and the construction and to get her to sea in twenty-four months.

Q: At that time, I understand, at least two years had been lopped off the original schedule?

Mr. S.: I don't know. Others would know that better. But we were faced with the job of doing the detailed design and getting in all the purchases and subcontracts, getting the whole thing together and to sea in twenty-four months. And the second boat was to follow it in thirty days. So speed was the essence. In addition, of course, to get it out fast and get it out right, otherwise there was no use in getting it out fast.

The Bureau had already hit on the idea of taking one nuclear attack submarine that we had started on the ways, cutting it in two, and using its fore part and its after part with a new, lengthened middle part.

Q: That was the Scorpion that was under way?

Mr. S.: I think that was the Scorpion. There were several of that class.

This was nothing new. Ships have been cut in half and lengthened many times. In fact I cut the submarine S-48 in half way back in 1924 and put in a longer middle body. That was a completed submarine. When you cut a completed submarine in half and open it up, it's like breaking a piece of celery. In pulling it apart all the electrical cables and pipe connections and everything else, all the nerves of the submarine, have to be severed.

Q: Doesn't this weaken a boat structurally?

Mr. S.: Not in the least. In those days, 1924, they were riveted hulls and you had to make sure there was no single belt of juncture, no single line of juncture. Modern submarines are built by joining cylinders and at the connection between each cylinder there is a continuous line of welding all around the circular hull, and the safety of that joint has long ago been established. So all you do is to cut a weld that was previously made, a circumferential belt, slide the two ends apart, and go on to put more cylinders in the middle to contain all the features special to the Polaris submarine.

Q: Did you know, at that point, how much space was going to be required?

Mr. S.: Oh, yes. The Bureau had progressed that far. The decision had been made by Raborn's crew and the team that they had from the other agencies, from the other parts of the Navy, as to how many missiles, the gross size, how much space for fire control, and each of the principal subcontractors had their areas cut out for themselves and defined closely enough to be able to set the over-all size and characteristics of the submarine. Therefore there was no lost time in doing the detailed design. As a matter of fact, I think the job done by the Raborn leadership, Special Project, and all the other Bureaus and principal subcontractors was absolutely outstanding because you can't name another job, except Apollo in these years, of equal complexity, that took the working together of so many separate entities, having everything fit and work together inside the rigidly confined limits of a submarine hull. The more difficult and the faster it was, the more effective the decisions were and the agreements and their execution.

It also bears out my lifetime experience in production, that if you want a thing done well, it's got to be urgent and it's got to be fast.

Q: There's got to be pressure!

Mr. S.: There's got to be pressure, and the more the better. Any routine job is not likely to be as well executed and the cost of a routine job, for my money, is bound to be more than that of a pressured job, even though the pressured job is worked overtime without stint, and although purchases or other minor decisions are made without trying to wring out the last nickel. Still, the over-all cost is, for my money, bound to be less than if it were done on a routine basis.

Q: In that respect, then, I suppose Sputnik was a blessing for us. It applied this pressure.

Mr. S.: Certainly. You couldn't do it under the routine checks and counterchecks of "business as usual." As a matter of fact, public business has come to the state where everyone has to be afraid of being criticized or later found not to have done a perfect job. You can't help but make some mistakes, but it's the batting average that counts. But these pressure jobs, and almost every one I've been in has been a pressure job, otherwise there was no fun in it, are the ones that really get executed in a high degree of effectiveness, quality, and cost. Well, I've said enough of that to give you the idea.

Q: Working under pressure like that, there must have been some missteps, were there? I mean, this was almost a pioneering effort.

Mr. S.: You suggested that over the phone. I can cite other jobs, more routine jobs, where there were serious missteps, but I've had trouble trying to recollect any on the Polaris. We had some initial problem on the building ways, in very cold weather, with cracks in the welding, but we've had that before, and in all these new submarines we were using a new steel, so-called HY-80, and we had to dig out the cracks and re-weld them. We had the same thing on other submarines.

Other than that, and you can't say that's a mistake, it was not having had experience enough under subzero temperatures in the preheating of this metal and its effectiveness, I don't know of a job that had fewer so-called mistakes to look back on and pinpoint. Which, again, I believe, bears out the fact that the higher the pressure, the better the job will be.

Q: From the outset, I take it, for you and for Electric Boat it didn't seem an impossible task, to turn out this submarine?

Mr. S.: Well, you don't stand around debating that. The powers that be and Red Raborn and all the way up in the Navy, they wanted to deploy these boats. They had the timetable set. We didn't have much chance to debate that. The main thing was to get going on it.

I think one reason that we got assigned the first two was that we had just completed the delivery of the second nuclear submarine, the Skate, in less than contract time. Nobody else had built or completed any nuclear submarines. So we had already shown that we could deliver on a fast basis.

Q: When the pressure on this project was applied did you have adequate personnel at Electric Boat to handle the new job?

Mr. S.: We had a lot of people. We expanded over the twelve years that I was there. We went up from about 2,000 people to about 12,000 or 13,000. I don't think we staged any specific new hiring program. Actually, we slackened off some on lesser priority jobs and we put the cream-of-the-crop personnel, both design and construction, into this job.

Q: Did it involve at the plant itself the idea of fragmentation, which Lockheed and others adopted? Did you also do this? I mean, did the segregate the Polaris project from the others in Electric Boat?

Mr. S.: Even before the Polaris project came, we really had project management for the several different types of contracts that we had. We had vertical direction of each project, each specific type. It was called project leadership, and there would be a single man upon whom you could put the finger as the head of that project, and we just set up another project for the Polaris submarines. We didn't have to change the structure of the yard, and according to priorities, Polaris had the highest priority so we put the best men we had on it.

Q: Did you sit in on any of the Saturday conferences down in Washington? Raborn had various people in constantly to report on progress.

Mr. S.: Yes.

Q: Tell me about some of those.

Mr. S.: They were masterpieces of a master leader. Raborn's whole philosophy of dealing with this conglomerate bunch of principal contractors was to get the top men and to have them thoroughly understand their job, and then to give them some scope, some rope, in executing it. He did not nitpick every detail, but he brought out the best in the contractors by getting them to understand his and the Navy's urgency, and getting a thorough understanding of their jobs and then giving them some chance to do it, instead of bothering them. These meetings were one of his ways, to pick the highlights, to search for problems if they weren't self-evident, put on some more pressure, and give each of the contractors a chance to see the other fellow's difficulties, because, particularly at Electric Boat where all these things came together, each one had to give a little to accommodate the other. You couldn't do an isolated job. It all had to fit together.

Counting top responsible men, not just helpers, I think we had over 150 subcontractors' people at the ship yard, on the boat or in the shops, overseeing their part.

Q: Were these contractors with whom you had dealt before?

Mr. S.: Mostly. General Electric was in, Westinghouse, Lockheed - we hadn't dealt with Lockheed before - various subcontractors. And it took something like Raborn's philosophy to get such a conglomerate bunch of individual contractors, supposedly each interested only in his own skin, in harness and get them all pulling together. I don't think the equal of this job has been seen.

Q: How was this accomplished?

Mr. S.: You've met Raborn. You know -

Q: Yes, but for the record, your interpretation of how it was.

Mr. S.: I'm not much good at that. I don't remember any hidden gripes of feelings of disagreement. All I ever felt, leaving that guy, was how much more I could do for him, how much more was there I could do for him. He left you with the feeling that you would do anything to bring his goals to a successful conclusion. He was a very inspiring leader.

I can tell you one little story. I don't think he would remember this himself. Either at one of the regular meetings or a special meeting - I went down frequently - he did have a bone to pick with me about something in connection with our work. He was tied up with a great many people, but he didn't keep me waiting too long, and it was close to lunchtime. He simply stated unemotionally what his views were on a certain thing and then - looking at his watch, he said:

"By the way, it's time to eat. Come on home with me."

I went to his quarters in the Washington Navy Yard and while Mrs. Raborn was putting on the lunch he sat down at the organ and just struck thunder and lightning out of that instrument. And when he got up, he said:

"Now you see how I feel and there's no need to talk about it any more."

He felt deeply about this thing from the way he stroked that organ. But he didn't keep on yammering.

That was a little example of Raborn's techniques.

Q: Pretty clever!

Mr. S.: He had a unique way of handling what would otherwise be a rough situation.

Q: This feeling that he generated in you and others to really exert yourselves to the utmost, did this percolate down to the men at Electric Boat?

Mr. S.: Oh, yes. Well, take a Navy boat. A ship goes as the captain on the bridge, whether it's got plenty of sap and will-to-do and wins a battle efficiency pennant or something else even aside from actual combat. The ship reflects the man on the bridge, and Raborn's personality and urgency inspired confidence in people. He got little fellows to do bigger things than they would ordinarily have done. He brought out the best in people. A very unique quality.

Q: He told me about going around the country to the various industries and assembling the workmen and their wives and telling them about this Polaris project, the urgency back of it, and the fact that it was absolutely necessary for their safety, the safety of the nation. Did he do this at Electric Boat?

Mr. S.: Yes. That's a most difficult thing to do, to enthuse a large number of people over a microphone. He was a master at it, but where he was absolutely unique was in person-to-person contact with a smaller group, where his dedication came across.

Q: Yes, it borders on flag-waving and borders on being a little bit corny and yet he managed to do it.

Shugg - 18

Mr. S.: That's right. I haven't got the words to say what it takes, but it takes what he had. Rickover's projects use the opposite technique. It at least proves there's more than one way to do anything.

Q: How frequently did you go to Washington to make your reports to Raborn?

Mr. S.: We had a formal report meeting at least once a month, but there were bang-bang meetings on any particular specific item. Probably a couple of times a month or more than that.

Q: Admiral Burke told me one time that the top leadership took the precaution at the outset of saying that there should be a cut-off of the entire project if it appeared to be on the point of failing, not being able to accomplish it. Did this come to the fore ever in any of those meetings you attended?

Mr. S.: I didn't even hear about it. It was never used as a threat. There were no threats in this business. At least, I never heard of any. There was no question of its not working. There was only the question of doing your part and the confidence that that the other fellows were doing their part. Everybody was going to do their part and the thing was going to work.

There were no threats. There was no stick - carrot only, and not a carrot in the cheap sense of the word, but a can-do-

Shugg - 19

plus attitude.

Q: You being the over-all boss at Electric Boat, what percentage of your time was consumed with Polaris at the height of this?

Mr. S.: Well, like any other management job, you put your time necessarily somewhat in the order of priority, and this was by far the top priority and it got immediate attention. We even stamped our purchase orders. We had a great big rubber stamp made, "This order is a part of and necessary to the Polaris program." That was flashed all over the front page of every purchase order, and everybody knew what the Polaris program was. This wiped away the usual alibi-ing and talk about conflict of interests with some other order or somebody being ahead of you. It worked all the way down the line of suppliers.

Q: How important was the element of security at Electric Boat for this project?

Mr. S.: You mean security in the sense of - ?

Q: Not revealing.

Mr. S.: - foreign intelligence?

Q: Yes.

Mr. S.: We already had a pretty tight security connected with the nuclear submarines, and I'm not conscious of any brandnew steps taken on account of Polaris. I don't think they had to be taken.

Q: So it was relatively easy for Electric Boat?

Mr. S.: Yes. This security business is not a mathematically determinable thing, you know. Take the Atomic Energy Commission where security was so important. One of the top men, Dr. Fuchs, at Los Alamos, defected and went over to the Russians. What good were all the guards and everything else? You still have to do it, but you might as well recognize that the real breaks in security come in a way that has nothing to do with the ordinary measures you take, and that's best illustrated by Dr. Fuchs walking off with more knowledge in his head than they could have found out by rifling an office.

That reminds me that when I came in from Hanford every month to Washington I had to carry a certain piece of data with me. I could have carried it in my head, I guess. It was classified "top secret." It was a certain figure each month, and finally one of the security men at the Washington office asked me if I was carrying a gun, and I said I was not. He said, well, for top secret data I should have a gun under my arm or somewhere, and I told him that was not for me. And he said:

"Well, we'll have to send an official courier with you." I said, "Help yourself," so the next time I came in an official courier comes out from Washington, with a gun, and with a briefcase with a big chain and padlock on it, which advertised its importance to anybody seeing it.

We had to change planes at Pendleton, Oregon, and our plane through to the East was late, so we went down town to a small lunchroom, and when the airport called - they were in touch with the plane - we went back to the airport and were sitting there, waiting for it to come in, when all of a sudden I saw this professional courier stiffen up in his seat and go white in his face, and I said:

"What's biting you?"

He said, "My God, I left that briefcase in the lunchroom!" So we got the manager of the airport to promise to hold the plane, if necessary, and we tore back down town in his car and the lunchroom was closed. But there was a white-aproned man cleaning it up and we banged on the door long enough so he let us in, and there was the padlocked, chained briefcase in the same stall that we'd been eating in!

So, I say what price official couriers? Enough of that.

Q: Tell me about Electric Boat's cooperation with Newport News and I guess it was Mare Island?

Mr. S.: Well, it's pretty obvious that the job was bigger than any one yard, and also from a pure physical security point of view. We had several active nuclear reactors, at one time at our piers. Although I personally think the danger is minimal -

suppose there had been some kind of an accident. We were the only ones in the business. I don't go for a single supplier in anything important, anyway. There should be some spreading of anything of that importance. And from a national, point of view we all felt it was right for others to be engaged in it. We knew we were tops anyway. We were the lead. The others built their submarines all from our plans. We were the lead yard and the way to get big in a job is not to monopolize it and hold on to it yourself, but to stay better than the others. And it was good for us to have competition. It sharpened some of these people up. It's a very good thing. Multiple sources of supply, you should have competition, and no complaints as long as we were the lead yard.

Q: Did you have to loan some of your trained personnel to these other yards?

Mr. S.: At various times we did.

Q: Because they were new to the atomic field.

Mr. S.: Yes. We did that at various times on the nuclear projects and also on the Polaris project.

Q: That leads me to a question about training personnel in this area. How did you go about this?

Mr. S.: Originally, at Electric Boat, for nuclear power aspects Admiral Rickover had enough experience training some staff of his own to insist that key men be picked and given a short course at Oak Ridge, at least to rub their noses into the over-all aspects of such a unique program. Also, we had Electric Boat design and build the land-based prototypes at Arco, Idaho, and at West Milton, New York, so that even the workmen had a chance to get their know-how through work on the land-based prototypes. The power plant at Arco was built to the same plans as its successor in the submarine. But the prototype in obviously a better way to train people directly on this job.

Rickover is very strong on training. He's done a great job on it. That's the best excuse he has for talking about education.

Q: Had you gone through the Oak Ridge routine yourself in order to know what your men were acquiring?

Mr. S.: No. What training I had I got by being jammed into the job at Hanford. At that time I was living alone and it was a night-and-day job of living with the work and with the men who knew the work, former Manhattan Project men and we got some DuPont men to come back. It wasn't formalized training, but it was training on the job.

Q: Tell me, Sir, about Rickover's role in this whole thing. He was in BuShips.

Mr. S.: Yes. Of course, Rickover's big ten strike was pushing through the first demonstration of nuclear propulsion. There isn't any question but that his ramrod techniques and passion for thoroughness was responsible for cutting several years, if not five years, off the actual successful demonstration of nuclear propulsion. That cannot be taken away from him. But you have to watch out that a tenstrike as big as he made doesn't result in later thinking that there's no other way, that that is the last word.

We can all name several big companies which didn't come alive again until the founder finally gave way to fresh blood.

Q: I suppose a primary example of that is the Ford Motor Company.

Mr. S.: Yes. Henry hung on to the Model-T too long. You can name as many as I can.

Any man, I believe, has two parts in a big task. One is to accomplish that big task well, and the other is to build up a gang that can carry on and keep it growing. Also, any such person is liable to be handicapped by the NIH philosophy "not invented here." That happens to the shop foreman and it happens to designers, it happens to you and me, and it can happen to an admiral. I just hope that the "not invented here" philosophy has not resulted in other possessors of this know-how from finding even new and better ways. Nothing stays the same. The first one cannot be forever the best one. It is bound to be improved upon.

Q: There again, the pressures are applied by our competitors. The Russians are going forward with techniques, so this forces us automatically.

Mr. S.: Sure. Obviously, they have a good technical outfit, as demonstrated by Sputnik. We got to the moon first, there's no question about that, but this is a see-saw between competitors.

Q: What role did Rickover play vis-a-vis Electric Boat in the development of Polaris?

Mr. S.: Rickover was not the first noteworthy party outside of Special Projects to climb aboard. Now, it's true, very obviously, that Rickover's development of nuclear propulsion made the vehicle for Polaris possible. Polaris could not have accomplished its mission with the former type of propulsion. So the fundamental vehicle ability of prolonged submergence was Rickover's contribution.

A vertical project agency had been set up for the Polaris program with Admiral Raborn as its head, and its accomplishments in developing a solid fuel missile, underwater launching, fire control, and overcoming the limitations of space and weight inside a submarine have not been surpassed - except, perhaps, by NASA in the outer space field.

Interview with Dr. Jack W. Dunlap

Place: His office in Darien, Connecticut

Date: Monday morning, 2 October 1972

Subject: Polaris Project

By: John T. Mason, Jr.

Q: It's great to be able to meet you, Sir. I've heard a little bit about you from Admiral Raborn and it's all borne out in this brief moment I've been with you.

In talking about the Polaris program, would you begin by telling me just a little bit about how you came to know Admiral Raborn and how he came to know your abilities and thereby got you involved in the Polaris program when it came along?

Dr. D.: I suppose that the real answer to that was the machinations of the Bureau of Personnel when they assigned me to aviation gunnery under the Bureau of Aeronautics which then was under the command of Lieutenant Commander Raborn.

Q: This was back in 194-?

Dr. D.: This was back in 1943. My duty there was to assist in the training and in the testing of equipment for training aviation gunners.

Q: So you were dealing with him then in that capacity?

Dr. D.: I worked directly under his command or orders. This involved developing tests for various types of equipment, such as the 3A-2 trainer, which was a movie projector for training gunners, the testing of gun sights, the evaluation of various types of equipment, and the procurement of equipment for use. He subsequently assigned me to Pensacola to work with the gunnery school and later on to the Jacksonville gunnery school where we carried out other experiments.

Q: Where had you acquired your technical knowledge, Sir? You are basically a psychologist, are you not?

Dr. D.: Well, that's a question. I have degrees in agriculture, economics, mathematics, statistics, and psychology - experimental psychology. Most of my graduate work was in mathematics and statistics, experimental design. And while I do have a Ph.D. in psychology but not in mathematics, that was a happenstance. I'd spent my life on design and experiments in developing statistical data for various problems. You applied these techniques to the evaluation of equipment, to various industrial problems, problems on reliability, problems on validity, and so forth.

Q: And your role was centered in Connecticut?

Dr. D.: No, Sir. My first job was done for the Navy in 1927 in the late fall at Pearl Harbor, where a young lieutenant who was in charge of the shops and shop personnel came to me at the University of Hawaii and asked me if there was any way he could test these green laborers from the cane fields to determine which had some mechanical aptitude.

We developed some tests there. They were quite crude, but they proved fairly effective for what he wanted. I have been a professor in Hawaii, at Fordham University, Columbia University, and the University of Rochester. I guess that covers that. Do you want any personal information, Sir?

Q: Yes.

Dr. D.: I've been the president of some seven or eight professional societies and editor of three technical journals, founded two professional societies, and have founded some seven businesses.

Q: That's an extremely interesting background, and it begins to focus when you had this duty with Admiral Raborn. Throughout the war you were under him in one sense or another.

Dr. D.: Most of it. The important thing in my case was that the Navy, either by design or by luck, put me in one assignment after another for which I had the technical background and interest.

Q: You were one of the happy set of circumstances!

Dr. D.: Very happy circumstances.

Q: Talents were fitted to duties!

Dr. D.: That's absolutely right. So I consider that one of the happiest periods of my life.

I reported to duty in September 1942. I was supposed to report to duty in 1941 but my papers had been lost. My first assignment as a line officer was to the Bureau of Medicine and Surgery to set up and control statistical techniques applied to the selection and training of aircraft pilots and certain other medical problems. Early in 1943 I was transferred as a line officer to the Bureau of Aeronautics in the Department of Aviation Gunnery, or Free Gunnery, under Lieutenant Commander Raborn, who subsequently rose to Vice Admiral.

Under Raborn's directions I carried out the duties that I mentioned earlier and had the pleasure of becoming a personal friend of his.

Q: During that time, I think you said, you were also involved with Admiral Louis de Flores, were you not?

Dr. D.: Yes.

Q: Will you tell me a little about him in action? He was a fabulous person in the Navy records.

Dr. D.: Yes, I had contact and worked with Admiral de Flores. I met him first in 1941 in connection with providing him certain recording equipment, which we had found useful at the National Research Council in our work in testing and training aviation pilots. Admiral de Flores, as you know, was head of the Special Devices Center over at 410 H Street in Washington, which was an old garage. It was here that all types of training devices were developed - for air warfare, undersea warfare, and surface warfare. It has since grown to be a very tremendous activity, not only for the Navy but for the other services and also for industry.

de Flores, as you may recall, was very energetic and had a very inquisitive mind - a go-go type of individual, always courteous and polite and thoughtful. Being around him was like standing near an emery wheel when steel is touched to it and sparks fly in all directions, which would excite you and the others who were with you. I found him a very fine man to work for and with. Of course, you know he was a pilot and he held the basic patents on ethyl lead.

Q: No, I didn't know that.

Dr. Dunlap, you said that after you finally succeeded in extricating yourself from the service when the war was over, you continued a personal friendship with Admiral Raborn. Do you want to recall anything that pertains to that period?

Dr. D.: While he was a captain he was placed in charge of the Talos-Terrier missile program. They had him in a small room by himself at the top of the Pentagon. As he said, "Why have they got a fly boy in here trying to do something in ordnance? I don't know a damned thing about it." I can recall saying to him, "I know that but I'll bet you in six months you'll know more about it than most of them," which was characteristic of him.

Q: Did you keep abreast of the development of these missiles?

Dr. D.: Yes, and Dunlap and associates worked on them. We participated in that program. At one time I believe Dunlap associates had worked on some aspects of more missiles than any other company in the world.

Q: The Polaris program got under way in late 1955, according to the records, and Admiral Raborn was summoned to Washington and given his assignment perhaps in December of that year.

Now, you got involved very shortly thereafter.

Dr. D.: Yes. Around the middle of January, I believe about the 20th, I'm in my office one day and the phone rang and it was Admiral Raborn on the phone. He said, "What in the hell do you mean by retiring?" So I said, "Well, I just wanted to open up positions for younger men."

"Well," he said, "you just get your arse down here this afternoon. We've got something very important."

I said, "Yes, Sir."

Q: This was retiring from the Naval Reserve?

Dr. D.: Yes. And I got my arse down there that afternoon because I didn't trust that he couldn't work some machination to get me put on active duty again.

Q: Did you suspect what he had in mind?

Dr. D.: I hadn't the faintest idea what it was, except that he said it was urgent. I went down and he told me something of this program, he asked me to serve on the steering committee - on the civilian steering committee for the Polaris submarine. It was much hush-hush at this time. There was a meeting, in February, if I recall, of the committee and subsequently we had numerous meetings, once a month at first, and then at two month periods.

Q: Having been summoned, you stayed in Washington?

Dr. D.: No. I returned, as soon as I knew what I had to do. He asked me to put together some ideas with regard to manpower, with regard to training, with regard to human engineering. Human engineering was a thing Raborn had been very strong for ever since our acquaintance back in BuAir where we were trying to design equipment and modify it so that a man could use them.

Q: Would you give me a good definition of human engineering?

Dr. D.: Human engineering is the art of establishing interfaces between men and equipment. This can be in terms of controls, in terms of the load of work, in terms of the display systems, or in terms of layouts of the equipment and personnel.

Q: Very good!

Dr. D.: At one of the very early meetings, after much discourse about how large the submarine would have to be, what it could draw, how large the vessels should be, how many there should be, what would be the problems with regard to navigation, what would be the problems with regard to development of liquid or solid propellants, among other things it was decided it would have to be solid propellants, which raised a whole series of problems of itself. The problems of range had to be worked out and the control systems for the range. Some people thought the submarines should only carry two missiles, some four, and one person had as many as thirty-six.

Q: How many were involved in this steering committee?

Dr. D.: There were about twelve people.

Q: And these were scientists?

Dr. D.: All top scientists, top engineers, people from big aircraft companies, from GE, from laboratores like Draper of MIT. The inertial navigation system, of course, was discussed among other problems. They voted. This was one of the most scientific demonstrations I've ever seen for establishing something. They simply took a vote and I suppose it's all you could do at that time and established that the Polaris complement of missiles would be sixteen.

Q: This committee meeting, since you were dealing with many things that were just ideas and nothing more, was in effect a kind of an informed brainstorming session, wasn't it?

Dr. D.: Yes, it was. That's exactly what was going on there. Fortunately, at that time, Raborn, who has a gift for getting able people together and for enthusiasm, had selected very early a Captain Levering Smith, now Admiral Levering Smith, who is, in my opinion, one of the ablest engineer-scientists that I have ever known. A great deal of the credit, in my opinion, for the success of this operation goes to Levering Smith who was ably backed up by the corps of engineers and officers that Raborn had put together. Raborn's genius, to me, lies in his being a visionary, his ability to find the right people and to drive them unmercifully while making them enjoy being driven. That is the genius of this man.

Q: But never lifting the pressure!

Dr. D.: Oh, never lifting the pressure. He runs you with a steel fist in a velvet glove. Fortunately, he can peel the glove off and be very rugged.

Q: And I suppose there were times when this was necessary?

Dr. D.: Yes. He had one other thing and that is an encyclopedic memory, so that what he'd been told he could remember and recall years later. You must be careful when you deal with the man because he'll throw it into your face. Levering Smith has the same ability. I've seen him call a man in a meeting, "That isn't what you said, Mr. ---, two years ago in August. Mr. Secretary, turn back to the August meeting and read what he said." I've seen more than one big scientist and engineer and vice president or president of a company embarrassed as hell. You had to be careful with both of those men.

Q: I'm glad to have that warning!

Dr. Dunlap, just a brief tangent. In January of 1956 the directive was to cooperate with the Army - the basic directive - with the development of Jupiter, but your consultations in the committee meetings were focused not on Jupiter but on a Navy Polaris?

Dr. D.: Well, it was focused on equipment that could be used aboard a submarine and which could sit dormant yet be instantly ready, and you couldn't do that with the Jupiter.

The problem was that the ships had to be re-designed, the whole CG's had to be changed, you had to consider every inch of space and pound of weight. Then you had to consider the quarters for the men, the control systems, layouts, and the workload each individual could do. For example, there was one set of equipment operated by one man with a time allotment of fifteen seconds. We set up simulated equipments and used the brightest man on our staff, yet not one man could do it under twenty seconds. I doubt if you would find many able-bodied seamen who were the equivalent of these men for quickness and sharpness, of the men used in the experiment. Result: We recommended that either they put a second man on or modify the equipment, even if the load had to be reduced on the man or the equipment. This is what I'm talking about as an interface.

Q: I see, yes. Well, who had determined the fifteen seconds interval prior to your experiment?

Dr. D.: Someone who designed the equipment and the operational layouts. We were also involved here in manpower problems. But to come back to your question. Ships had to be re-designed, the right sort of solid propellants developed, range systems developed, an inertial navigation system designed and there were difficult communications problems to be solved. How many times in a day could you allow the sub to broach and at what hours. So, there was a plethora of problems, many of which had never been touched before and required starting from scratch.

To me, the fact that the first darned Polaris submarine and the first Polaris missile worked falls in the realm of magic. It just couldn't be done, it was an impossible assignment. Except for one minor detail, it worked pretty darned well. I remember on Polaris-1, when she first commenced to fire down range, we were firing at approximately 1,000 miles, and it was unbelievable how near the target these missiles were hitting. When you plotted them out you found that they were in a very close pattern. The biggest trouble I had expected would be with cross winds and thus your big dispersion would be lateral. It turned out that the biggest dispersion was vertical, i.e., down range.

It was also a shock to learn that starting with the pickle barrel they kept this dispersion within a three-quarter of a mile radius and most of them were in closer. I don't care how many megatons you put in there, I don't want to be three-quarters of a mile away from it, even with one of them going off!

Q: How frequently did this committee of twelve continue to meet, once you got under way?

Dr. D.: At first we met every month, and that went on for nearly two years. They also had a command room in which they had layouts of all sorts of information. In addition to these regular meetings of the committee there were other meetings of his staff. Dr. Talcott and I had to attend those meetings, too. These were progress reports, and this was where the PERT system was first developed.

Q: The what?

Dr. D.: P-E-R-T. That's simply a technique for developing a sort of flow chart to tell you when a piece of equipment will be ready, how long is it going to take, so when should one start, if this one is going to take two years to develop another equipment which can be accomplished in six months. One doesn't have to start at the same time. He can wait, let's say, fifteen months to develop the smaller equipment so that they come out and merge at the same time. This is the PERT system which in a modified form is widely used in industry.

I was responsible for providing S.P personnel with human engineering consultants. These men worked directly with the various SP groups in Polaris. They also made trips to various plants where human engineering groups had been established by companies to be sure that these people were coordinated with the overall work. That is the general role Dunlap & Associates had in the Polaris program.

When Admiral Raborn first requested H.E. personnel I told him I thought five people would be enough, if they were good men. He said, "You'd better make that twelve when you send them here." I was wrong because ultimately I think we had some eighteen or twenty men.

Q: To pursue one idea you mentioned here about the human engineering groups that were in existence within certain industries . . .

Dr. D.: No, they were not in existence. They were put into existence. In fact, some of the best men we had on our staff were hired away to head these up and develop them for these companies.

Q: You imply, then, that this was an entirely new technique for industry? These human engineering groups?

Dr. D.: For all practical purposes, yes. The human engineering work - I'll have to go back here. I became interested in this problem in 1923. This interest stemmed from my observations of where controls were placed on tractors and automobiles. For example, I had one Ford in which the hand brake was on the right-hand side and then subsequently one on the left-hand side and I had a hell of a time adjusting myself to it. I found an old Monroe calculator where it had been set up for business, i.e. two rows of white, three rows of black, and so on and so forth. But for the research man, the mathematician, statician, you wanted it in hundreds rather than in cents, you see. The simplest solution was to pull the caps off and shift them around so you could identify hundreds and thousands readily.

From such simple observations I became interested in the general field of layouts of controls whether you could see things; controls and sensor informations. This carried over later to the problems in airplanes, reading lights, the use of red light at night to protect the visual purple in the eye, etc.

Interestingly enough, the military were more interested in this in World War II than anyone else. This probably was due to the fact that a number of scientists in uniform recognized this class of problem.

Q: The whole scientific world virtually was brought in that way.

Dr. D.: After the war you tried to convince industry of this and the engineers would look at you and laugh and say, "What do you mean, human engineers? Do you mean to tell me I'm not a human?" But gradually this changed. A great deal of the change, by the way, can go back to an assignment given Dunlap & associates by Navy, to determine where and how human engineering could be useful. This study was in part stimulated by Raborn's interest in the whole field, so he has been a strong advocate for H.E. As a result, specs for the last twelve years - Air Force army and Navy specs - specifically state on the development of new equipment that the human engineering aspects shall be considered.

Q: Interesting.

Dr. D.: At the time Polaris started it was very seldom that you found anyone in industry interested in H.E. About 1951 Dunlap Associates began to put on human engineering seminars, and, interestingly enough, companies sent engineers. They came with a sneer and scoffing, but most of them left as converts. So companies commenced to add H.E. I think in the original days they sent their men because they just didn't want to miss out on something that might have some value, and it didn't cost too much to send a man to a week seminar.

We've since put on innumerable seminars for the military.

Q: Do you hold them here in Darien?

Dr. D.: We used to. We now hold them out in the field. We put one on in Washington or on the West Coast, wherever the military wants it.

Q: But this is post Polaris?

Dr. D.: Pre- Polaris that we were giving the seminars. This is in answer to your question, was industry prepared for this type of thing? No, it was just, here and there, that a man would become interested in it, and that was due, I think, in part, to the seminars. So when the Polaris program broke and Raborn insisted companies have a human

Dunlap - 18

engineering group. He put us in to see what they were doing and to coordinate their work because he didn't want one group doing this and another group doing that.

Q: This all tied in with the time schedule for the development of Polaris?

Dr. D.: That's right.

Q: Do you want to talk a little about that as a part of the steering committee? What voice did this group have in the development of the time schedule?

Dr. D.: Well, they had a considerable voice in the development of the schedule. Of course, the schedule had to be modified. They took these various progress reports and then frequently raised a question whether it could be done in the time set up on the PERT chart, and occasionally demanded it to be done faster. This was checked at the SP conferences, rather than at the over-all project conferences, but they did keep track of it and put pressure on.

Q: How did the time schedule come into being? Was it expedited by Sputnik? What was it that caused it to be such a . . .

Dr. D.: As I recall, the time schedule that was given to Polaris was that they were to have the Polaris submarine and missiles in operation in seven years, that is, 1955 to 1962 as an outside limit. Thus from the very beginning everyone was cognizant of time, but also was cognizant that if it could be done faster it should be. As you know, they did it two years ahead of schedule. All I can say is that there was really a gung-ho effort, somewhat analogous to the effort and drive that people put in at the beginning of World War II.

Q: It was, in effect, a crash program, wasn't it?

Dr. D.: Oh, yes. It took top priority over everything. What Polaris wanted, Polaris got. It had priority over all the other programs, so far as I know.

Q: The urgency, then, I take it, was a great factor in accomplishing it?

Dr. D.: Yes. The urgency was a great factor and that urgency was aided and abetted by one Red Raborn. He drove us like nobody's business. He cajoled us. He scolded us, and he whopped us once in a while. It was his ability to get people to go all out clear down into people in the plants. He was on the road a great deal and would go into a plant and talk to the workers there. He could get people that just ran a fork truck gung-ho. It's a wonderful talent. I'd rather have that than be bright!

Q: Tell me, Sir, when Dunlap Associates got their Polaris contract, how soon after the beginning of this concerted effort?

Dr. D.: You want the exact time?

Q: Well, the approximate time.

Dr. D.: We went to work at once, before we had the contract. We were told to. I went down there in the middle of January. I think it was April when we officially started to work. And the contract was just rammed through.

Q: In the human engineering aspect of your contract, you did send men out into industry, didn't you?

Dr. D.: Oh, yes. They were out into industry, to work with H.E. groups in industry.

Q: And you say over-all there were about 30,000 contracts and subcontracts?

Dr. D.: As I recall, there were 33,000, and I think we got the Polaris flag primarily because of Raborn and Levering Smith.

Q: Yes. In the book that Red Raborn approves of heartily The Adventure in Partnership, which you know, the statement is made that the success of it was due to the fact that we had a nationwide team in operation and one central force was a deep and a selfless motivation.

Dr. D.: Oh, that was another thing. This was a Holy Grail deal.

Q: How did that Holy Grail attitude develop? How was it generated?

Dr. D.: I don't know how he did it. Of course, everybody was worried about the communists at that time. That was really hot, and this was necessary, and if we didn't have something like this we'd probably be going down the drain. Those long-range missiles out of Russia, required us to have some way to counteract them. And, of course, there was a lot of glamor to it. This was at sea, we were going to operate undersea. It was impossible to detect these submarines. They could go from here to there, and we had circles drawn, radii, of how far out and what you could hit, how close in you could go, and then you could back up. This gives you a tremendous advantage. Now they've got it so that you can stand out 5,000 miles off the seacoast, nearly 5,000. They have a 5,000-mile radius.

Q: Can you in any sense compare the development of this Holy Grail quest attitude with the attitude which prevailed in World War II? Was there a similarity?

Dr. D.: In World War II, as you will recall, after Pearl Harbor there was a deep anger that stimulated people. There was the concept of treachery which they didn't like. So people in World War II were out for revenge, as well as self-preservation. In the concept of Polaris, here is something with which we're going to protect the world and the United States from destruction and this really is a mission. It isn't here now. This was like a crusader deal to save the world, and particularly save us from a mess like we got into in 1941.

Q: In this same book I referred to, it says that modifications within the industrial organizations themselves were required in order to maintain the pace set for every phase of delivering the weapon system, and probably the most important one was the concept of projectizing Polaris. Would you elaborate on that?

Dr. D.: You mean breaking it down in sub-projects?

Q: Yes, I guess that's it.

Dr. D.: Well, that's true. They broke it down really into components such as the inertial navigation system, etc. The reason this could work required a very tight command control over each element. This is why the center was set up, and PERT charts developed.

Otherwise, if you didn't have this very tight command and control situation, components would not be delivered on schedule. Further, each contractor would tend to build his thing bigger or slower, or this, that, and the other, and thus get more money. You had to keep them pulling together. You can't let a contractor build a piece of gear that's going to take up all the space available. One has to have other pieces of gear in the space. Granted, you can make me a bigger one and a better one and so on and so forth, but it is still no go.

That's about all I can tell you on that.

Q: Now, this projectizing was also typical within our industrial society?

Dr. D.: Yes, because they were forced. They had to make a PERT chart of all that they were doing, and Polaris had copies. When I speak of Polaris, I'm talking about SP-20. SP knew what was going on, they could look at the charts and if not on schedule demanded, how come? This resulted in some very rough and rugged sessions.

Q: Yes, this must have occasioned much reorganization within an industry like General Electric.

Dr. D.: Oh, yes. They had to set these up as special departments or special units.

Q: This entailed additional expense, personnel and what have you?

Dr. D.: Some personnel had to be added. Take Stan Burriss at Lockheed as an example. He was pulled in from another assignment and put into Special Projects work because he had certain experience years ago at Los Alamos. He was with Lockheed at the time so they put him on this and others above him. Stan did his assignment very, very well.

Q: As you have observed the scene since Polaris, has this technique been continued within industry? Have they continued to projectize when they're working on specific things?

Dr. D.: I know some instances. I don't know how widely it's used because I have not had a wide enough contact with industry. I do know that it has been followed by the Navy in some cases, too.

Admiral Goodfellow with this new class of ships is developing a very similar project or type of project, and Goodfellow was with Raborn in the early days. They had some extraordinary people there. I remember this Commander Bob Wertheim, an extraordinary man.

Q: Raborn said that in his opinion an effort of this sort had to be somewhat unique in order to be successful and it had to be a solo thing, that it would not have been possible if there had been two or three special projects under way simultaneously of different natures.

Dr. D.: Well, of course, this was the first, but the one thing that made it possible was that it carried top priority. That's what gave it the zip. He could get the money, he could get things done he wanted done and had to be done.

Q: And didn't have to conform to government procedures?

Dr. D.: Not the usual form. He had freedom to cut through much of the red tape.

Q: The awarding of contracts and so forth?

Dr. D.: Yes. On money and things of this sort, he needed it and he got it. Of course, luck had a lot to do with it in terms of the state of the art at which he came in, so it was often not too difficult to push the state of the art into hardware.

Q: You mean that a lot of spadework had been done?

Dr. D.: Yes. A lot of theoretical work and technical work had been done and thinking about these things, and the right people with the right training were available. That's what I meant about the luck. You had this spadework done, so that it was possible to make a project like this go. I think part was good luck, part was the leadership that the program had, part was the quality of the name naval officer they were able to draw on. Don't belittle those naval officers in any sense. They were very devoted, very intelligent, and very able men, technically and otherwise. But in industry, as I say, the state of the art had gone so far that much of the basic spadework had been done.

Q: You must have had yourself a good feeling. I mean you spoke earlier about in the early 1950s having pushed the idea of experimentation with intense heats and so forth. Well, a certain amount had been done in that area and you must have felt good about that.

Dr. D.: Yes, there was a little. We had a hell of a time, as you know, on the re-entry problem. We didn't know whether we were going to be able to get those first Polaris missiles down without burning up. They tried all sorts of things for the nose cone. They tried molybdenum, but that's a very heavy metal and, thus, when you did you had to change the whole configuration of the firing pattern and the range and how you made your settings and so on and so forth. Furthermore, molybdenum could burn out, sometimes, so the engineers finally came up with the idea of using an ablative form carbon. This raised problems of cracking. It was difficult to manufacture. But they mastered the production technique.

Q: In that account a point is made about the Milestone effort. I mean step by step.

Dr. D.: Yes, the milestones were set up and actually shown on the PERT charts which showed how much progress to date. That's a milestone. In fact, the Navy has since broadened this. They use milestones on many of their contracts and pay you according to whether or not you meet the milestones. A milestone is just a certain amount of work done at a certain level at a given point in time.

Q: Whose concept was this to apply to the Polaris program?

Dr. D.: I do not know.

Q: Was it tossed around in the Committee of Twelve?

Dr. D.: No. That could have come from almost anybody. I wouldn't be surprised that it came from Levering Smith.

Q: And a concommitant thing, the cut-off possibility which I understand somebody like Admiral Burke insisted upon - that there be certain stages in the development of this when it would be possible to cut off the project entirely and say that's it, we're not going any farther?

Dr. D.: I don't know about that. I do know this, though, and it's an important thing here. This was because the Polaris had such a high priority. You could award duplicate or triplicate contracts for a given job up to a given point. For example, let's take the inertial navigation system. They could give Jones a contract, and another to Smith and so forth, up to a certain point to see whose work was coming thru. Then they might only give two contracts for the next stage, and for the final stages only give it to one.

Q: But initially all three knew that they were vying with the others?

Dr. D.: Oh, yes. You had redundancy, but you couldn't be sure in the beginning which contractors ideas were the best. You had no way of telling, so you may have bet on the wrong dog. So they would take them all to a certain stage of development and then look at them and say, well, this guy has floundered out over here. Then you've got two left, so you set another "mile post" for them.

Q: When you're awarding, say, the initial three contracts

you're doing it on the basis of nothing more than just a concept of something you want?

Dr. D.: Well, a concept and what your own technical people in Polaris or special projects conceive as the soundest. You may have a dozen people and you pick out three. This is because you yourselves have some ideas and experience. Some proposals have readily apparent flaws. The Polaris team had to go through and evaluate every proposal and this was a terrible job.

Q: You're putting a great burden on the shoulders of a particular industry and the knowledgeable men there to implement the idea?

Dr. D.: Knowledgeable men in special projects. You see, they do the evaluation of these various proposals that come in, and say they've got ten and they're going to pick three. This is a technique in redundancy which you have to do when you are in a hurry and trying to break entirely new ground. This is what they had to do, they did it and, did it well. You found out which contractor couldn't stay up to his PERT charts, you found out which ones turned out to have some basic flaws which weren't apparent either to your side or theirs. There were a lot of things. Maybe you had the good luck and found one and where the project went through faster than you thought and the results were even better than expected at that stage. SP was very happy when that occured.

Q: You smiled at that!

Dr. D.: This happened.

Q: They did happen?

Dr. D.: Oh, yes.

Q: Were there any particular awards for such industries?

Dr. D.: I do not know. You see, I have always looked upon my role in life as to work and get things done and I'm not much interested in whether you put some little ribbons here or whether you pay me. I'm just interested in getting things done.

Q: But, as a psychologist, you do know that this is an important factor when dealing with human beings?

Dr. D.: Oh, yes. I admit this. I'm just saying that people differ in what they consider their value systems. My values are somewhat different.

Q: This is an area that no one has talked about: the whole aura of urgency and so forth, where this was a national challenge, had been established. But still were there not problems in terms of labor relations when you were dealing with so many industries?

Dr. D.: There must have been. I'm not familiar with that. I recall no serious labor problems though, which affected this particular program. I wouldn't want to have it said that I'm 100 percent correct, but I don't recall any major slow-down due to labor problems in this particular project. There must have been some, probably in some of the smaller components' areas.

Q: The steering committee and Raborn himself had established this go-go attitude.

Dr. D.: Everybody connected with this program, the Presidents of the companies and everybody else, were firmly convinced, as I said, that this was do or die. It's an extraordinary thing. I think it deserves write-up, not because of who was in it but because when men felt the urgency they could work together and really develop things ahead of time. It was a truly selfless program.

Q: Yes, and it was team work. This is the thesis that Raborn insists upon. Did you in your association with it have anything to do with some of the higher officials of government like, say, Secretary Wilson or even the President?

Dr. D.: Not at my level. I leave that to the big shots. I preferred Raborn to be the front for this. Now, it's true that I suspect some of the top men like those in Lockheed had contacts there, but I am not in a position to state, except I know Raborn did all the time. Who was this white-headed old Congressman from the House?

Q: Vinson?

Dr. D.: No, not Vinson. He's the MC who got everything in the world for the Charleston area.

Q: Mendel Rivers?

Dr. D.: Yes, and in some way Raborn had him in his hip pocket.

Q: He was an important man to have in his pocket! How long were you then and Dunlap Associates related to the Polaris project? How long did you continue?

Dr. D.: About six years.

Q: You saw it through its - ?

Dr. D.: Oh, completely through. Most of the subs were in the water and operating. We were in there until 1962 or 1963.

Q: This was after Raborn ceased to be in charge of it. I certainly want to thank you very much, Dr. Dunlap.

Interview with Gordon O. Pehrson

Place: Apartment of J. B. Colwell, Washington, D.C.

Date: Tuesday afternoon, 5 February 1974

Subject: Polaris

By: John T. Mason, Jr.

Q: Mr. Pehrson, I have heard a great deal about you, highly touted as a genius, and I am ready to recognize that fact because of what you've done for the Polaris program and other things.

Would you give me just a thumbnail on your background, on your career, before you entered into the Polaris effort?

Mr. P.: Well, you're tapping my memory on Polaris after the intervening fourteen years. I left that program in 1961 and now you're asking for antecedents to that period in time! It's fairly sharp in my memory because it was quite deliberate.

I went to the University of Minnesota in the early 1930s and I graduated in 1937, which was a very exciting time to be in a university because they were turbulent times and we challeneged the texbook dogmas by simply reading the headlines, especially in the economics field. My majors were in business administration and in government administration. I followed that work with a two-year scholarship under a Rockefeller grant in public administration and came to Washington as a part of something that was then known as the National Institute of Public Affairs. That was a fourteen-year program set up with Rockefeller money to bring graduates from various universities to Washington, slot them into what were called internships in various government spots, and, hopefully, they would do something to improve the career service of government.

Q: That's something that has been elaborated upon today?

Mr. P.: Yes. It lasted for about fourteen years and became a part of the Civil Service program. I think they call them junior assistants or something now and they are on the pay roll. But we were all in as dollar-a-year men. We were living on our scholarships. It was a very stimulating program.

Then I decided that government was an area in which one could follow any interest and many interests. I sort of divided in my own mind the functions of the government. Not too elaborate, but it was conscious. I moved from my internship in the Department of the Treasury into a relief program because I became interested in federal-state relationships programs, and then became an assistant director of a research and records program in the State of Virginia, under the well-known WPA administration. I don't know whether you go back that far.

Q: Yes, indeed. The Blue Ridge Mountains.

Mr. P.: Yes. I covered that state like a blanket. We set up an interest in an organization there, courthouses and mostly of the cities and counties' authorities. Then, after we got that set up, I got interested in another function of government, which was the regulatory function and had a choice of going with the National Labor Relations Board or something else. I became a little conservative at that time and decided on one of the more conservative programs, which was the Federal Deposit Insurance Corporation, the banking side, which was a new regulatory role of the federal government.

Q: That had been established by Herbert Hoover!

Mr. P.: That's right, and Crowley was head of that group at that time. I worked the southern states out of Atlanta for a number of years. The war came along. In the meantime I'd got married, and was attracted to a third federal government activity, which was the investigatory functions, the choice being things like the FBI and so on. There was great expansion of Civil Service at that time. Pearl Harbor recruits and so on. So I became a federal investigator with a Civil Service commission, which was

Q: A wide spectrum of experience!

Mr. P.: Yes. It was very exciting work actually. It was the best course in human psychology that I could have taken. It was much better than learning how to
A lot of it comes from cynicism, that nobody can stand an investigation. Another cynical observation is that if you want to find out what's wrong with a person, talk to his best friends, but didn't become completely cynical as a result of that experience.

I entered the Navy as an ensign in the Supply Corps, did three years' duty in the South Pacific, etc. Came back —

Q: Where were you based in the South Pacific? Manus?

Mr. P.: No. I was about ready to go to Manus. We were in the Russell Islands, on an island called Banika, north of Guadalcanal. We moved from there not to Manus — part of our gang went to Manus, the rest of us went up to Mindoro, in the Philippines. Got back from that experience the day they dropped the bomb on Hiroshima, and got out of the Navy six months later.

I looked to new fields in federal activity, still on my learning curve, as it were, as to what governments can do, and got involved with the very large, growing program at that time, which was the Veterans Administration. This was a new agency, obviously to take care of the World War II veterans, and we had all the growing problems of setting up a field apparatus. I got into that at one of the branch levels - Dallas, which covered Texas, Mississippi, and Louisiana - in the coordination and planning group. Moved from that into a hospital administrative role as a hospital supervisor for those three states, and then recommended or participated in studies that recommended the abolition of our branch after we'd set the thing up and in the process found myself without a job.

I wanted to come back to Washington anyway. I'd been in the boondocks long enough. Came back to the central part of the government where one could find out where the major program decisions were made which, of course, is the Bureau of the Budget, so I became a budget examiner working on Navy appropriations mainly.

Q: I notice in that earlier period a strong strain of social service.

Mr. P.: Well, not in a humanitarian sense. I was interested in the people I worked with. I was very interested in how these things are managed. I'm not going to get too philosophical here, but I did my graduate on what I thought was a very interesting subject, the only hope of a democracy is efficient and effective and responsible bureaucracy. That's how I got my scholarship to Washington. I felt it then and I still feel it. No comment on how those hopes and ideals have been prejudiced by the behavior here in Washington for the last couple of years, because they've been a complete 180° away from what I and many of the people who came to Washington in the 1930s believed in. A responsible as well as an effective and efficient bureaucracy. Bureaucrat was not a dirty word with us. It suffers by comparison with the reputation of the British Civil Service on one point. I guess that one point is the word "respect." Over there, the civil servants of the British government are respected and in this country they are not. Maybe they shouldn't be, but everybody in the service ought to be working towards respectability, which includes the element of being responsible to a constituency, which doesn't vote for you but nevertheless you have a responsibility to behave that way in your authority.

A week before the Korean War, which would have been 1950, June, I was offered a position in one of the bureaus that I was examining as a budget examiner, the Bureau of Ordnance.

Q: And that's where you met J.B.?

Mr. P.: Yes. Admiral Chuck Noble was the chief of the bureau and he'd heard some place that "I can't beat you, so would you join me." It's pretty hard to turn down that kind of an appeal, so I joined him as his chief budget officer, and we had an interesting experience there in terms of Navy appropriations to support the Korean War. The delightful surprise that came at the end of a year was that the captain who was the comptroller was relieved of duty and I was called in and offered the job, which was really quite a shock because the "Gun Club" in the Navy is the most military of all the services, and to put a civilian into a military billet that was rather prestigious at the time was a sort of shock. I think there were some admirals who rolled over in their graves when they found out about it.

Q: Albeit, you had a bit of a naval background, in supply!

Mr. P.: Yes, I had a Navy background, one could say, but I didn't have any good sea stories, except the ones one sees in the right books.

This was a marvelous time to get involved in Navy business and to begin for the first time to associate myself with Navy people. I'd been counseled by all my civilian counterparts, don't go into the Navy, the brass down there will bury you! So, I had half-humorously collected two titles for a book I was going to write - or two books I was going to write. The first one was "Life Behind the Brass Curtain," and the other one would have been "The Life of Red Tape," which would have recounted my frustrations.

Q: But you never arrived at the point where you'd written these?

Mr. P.: No, I've never written to those titles and I've never had any reason to even think about it because of the marvelous exposure of extremely competent and dedicated people.

Well, we're now in the Navy Department.

The Army was being reorganized about that time for the umpteenth time. They were setting up a new command structure in the supply area, consolidating several technical services of the Army under a Deputy Chief of Staff for Logistics, and they offered me the position of top civilian in that group, to head up something they called the Business and Industrial Management Office. I took that position under General Palmer, enjoyed a year of struggling through that particular kind of organization.

Q: Was it innovative work?

Mr. P.: I tried to make it so, although General Palmer was appointed Assistant Chief of Staff of the Army and they brought in a sort of a rough, bluff, combat officer from Korea and put him in the program. He hadn't any use for civilians and I found myself subordinated to a brigadier general who was a favorite friend of this man. They gave me a new title and assigned me to limbo in a sense. But, yes, there was the possibility for being innovative. We brought in some very interesting ideas there. General Palmer was one of my great supporters and I shared this information with his talent.

I'd been there a month when he called me into his office and said: "OK, Pehrson, you're a hot shot [Navy]. What's wrong with the Army?"

Well, I'd scarcely   in my little office but if you're going to be asking me questions, I'll give you my kind of an answer. "The way you're trying to run the seven technical services based on four assumptions, all of them are wrong, and if they are all right, your fifth assumption, which is the important one, is wrong." And if you know General Palmer you'll know I'm quoting him quite correctly when he said: "What the hell are you talking about, Pehrson?"

So I told him. I said:

"You are assuming in running your seven technical services and your supply depots and arsenals and all the rest of it, that there is a best single way to do everything. You're assuming that you've got somebody smart enough to find out what that best single way is, that you have the skills to describe what that best single way is and document its   and that you've got people out there on the receiving end of these orders who will obey them.

"Now, if all of those assumptions were correct and you could do these four things, then your fifth assumption is that when the balloon goes up your whole organization is going to respond and create an imaginative problem-solving terms, after having lived under that kind of a disciplined condition for all of these years."

He said: "I see what you're driving at, but prove it."

So I went in next door and filled up a coffee cart with Army regulations and procedures. They made a ten-foot shelf, and I said, "This is what I'm talking about. You've got a regulation on everything from where does the commanding officer keep the key to his safe to what time of the day is he permitted to go to a latrine. And it's flat wrong. The right answers are not here, and you haven't found them if they were here."

I'm responding to your question as to whether it was creative. Yes, we had a lot of fun.

Q: Did he retaliate by saying, "Well, what about the Navy?"

Mr. P.: No, he never did that. He wasn't that kind of a person. He looked at this thing not in relative terms but in absolute terms, and said "What do we do about it, you make us sound pretty horrible."

So, we did quite a bit about it in a year's time, eliminated report after report after report, changed the regulations. We tried to make independent people or tried to create managers to build some sense out of what I choose to call the command-management system. The military's got a tremendous advantage over private industry because it does have a command structure, and if you can build good management principles around the strength of that command structure, you can do tremendous things.

Q: All the discipline that goes into it?

Mr. P.: Yes, and the people will respond, you see. In industry, if you don't like the way the management is behaving you can quit, get another job, or something. Well, there are some constraints on that and there's a rationale to the command system which, if you feed the right management information through it and use it the right way, it becomes a plus. Of course, if you don't put the right management philosophy to work in this case, then it becomes very much of a minus because your command structure dictates behavior and if it's the wrong behavior there's no self-correcting device that will apply. But looking at it on the positive side, as we tried to do and we did in the Polaris activity - there we had a command management system that worked. I cannot minimize the fact that there was a command element to that. There was an admiral and captains are subordinate to an admiral. They may have questioned some of the things they did, but they started off by accepting it, you see, and the proof that it was wrong became their responsibility, not his, which is not always the case in private industry.

Well, anyway, in 1956 or 1957 -

Q: 1956 is when you came to the Polaris project, early in 1956, and there was some problem of getting you over there, was there not?

Mr. P.: Not really. You know the grade structure in the Civil Service. I was a grade 17 in the Army, so-called super grade, and Raborn didn't have any positions set up at all and he certainly didn't have any at that level.

There was a fellow named Ed Mernone, a civilian little fellow. You might want to talk to him because there were three people who set that thing up as so-called charter members, who were the original plank owners. They were Raborn, Hasler, Captain Hasler, and Mernone. Bill Hasler was on missiles in the Bureau of Ordnance and he had sort of been given the job of designing an organization for the SP. Ed Mernone was a civilian working in Research and Development division of BuOrd, on the budget side, a very capable, bright, energetic young fellow. He has aged, as we all have, but he's in town.

I think those were the three original people and, of course, very shortly after J.B. came in as the deputy and started recruiting staff.

Mernone had the job of working his way through the Civil Service Commission in getting any kind of jobs described. He was familiar with that procedure. He had to describe the job and he had to get them classified. There are people in that personnel field who make a living out of being difficult, to make a somewhat unfriendly observation.

Q: Who live by the book of rules!

Mr. P.: Yes.

Q: They're inflexible!

Mr. P.: You get more cynical. There was a Civil Service classifier and, if in the process of finding out what the job the person described and wanted classified - if, in the process of doing that, he decided that he could do that job himself, he would never allot a rating to it higher than his own! I think he was about a 12 or something, so nobody ever got above a 12 without a long-drawn-out discussions. But Mernone and Raborn were tremendously precisive in all areas, and they worked a deal with the Civil Service Commission where they sent two of their top classifiers from the Civil Service Commission, sat them down in the space that we had over there, and I think they turned out about two job descriptions every hour or every two hours, which was fantastic because they mull over these words as though they were building some exotic piece of furniture for weeks or months. But they were turning things out and, in the process, they got the kind of a super grade that I had had. I made a lateral transfer, which in the way those things happen in the Civil Service was almost like a hurricane.

Q: When you went there, they had what's known a Plans and Policy Division already set up, did they not?

Mr. P.: I should know that, but I really don't. I think probably they'd conceptualized the organization in terms of four parts – three parts, really. There were the director and the deputy, then there was administrative bureau, somebody to do the housekeeping sort of things, but the main structure of the Special Project office, I think they had conceived of it as being divided into what would be a technical director with subdivisions related to the hardware of the weapon system. They may have set everything else aside and called it plans and policy, but I had the impression - it's ridiculous for me not to know precisely, but I think I probably designed my own three branches. Whether I designed them or not, I adopted them because they made sense, and it was unique in the sense that it permitted a complete marriage of what were called comptroller functions with planning functions.

In the structure of the military departments at the highest levels the comptroller is always the staff group set aside from people making planning decisions or even getting too much involved in meaningful review of missions, which is one of the horrible things that have happened. They haven't changed it, but in this one we set up these three, it was called SP 10, and I took the planning function and had the opportunity, although it was challenged, to use military people in the function that military people should be used for, namely, offering military judgments. Not judgments of military people, but military judgments. One of the banes of a civilian's existence in the military departments is running into a military person who offers opinions on the procurement, research and development, anything, and he tries to add to his opinion the weight of its being a military opinion, and it's not a military opinion. It's sometimes difficult for those people.

On the other hand, the military judgments on this weapon system had to come from military people. I wasn't going to clobber up that function with a ~~trained~~ bunch of trained or intellectually bright civilians.

Q: What was your broad commission, as you came over? What were you charged with?

Mr. P.: I think it described itself into three branches, as it was finally set up. There was that planning function. We had to lay out the program plans, not the technical plans but the program plans. We were chartered to create a military capability not just to build a missile or to build a submarine that would fire a missile, but to create a complete military capability. And the principal function of my planning group was to ensure that we had defined and dimensioned our program so that it would in fact, if successful, give us a new kind of capability.

The work that we did in our planning divided itself into three basic areas: one was the hardware, the ship, the missile, the launcher, the navigation system, fire control, and so on; then there were the men, this whole problem of recruitment - it involved that, the training and getting ready of the men, and taking care of the men who were working on this hardware; and then there was the third area, which involved logistic support, which was the means, whether it was communications equipment, the main, or the tenders, or the magazines, which were set up at Charleston - the whole array of things that made it possible for men and machine to get together to a point of military application.

This became the program, and it was the planning function to ensure that we included as much in this definition of what was a complete ballistic-missile program as was required to create a capability. So that's, in a sense, where the people that told us why we existed and where we were going. I'll use simple terms now.

The next group I call the review group - well, I'll go back. The other one was the resources group. They were the group that was supposed to tell us what we needed to get from where we were to where the planning group said we wanted to go. It was resources in terms of money, to some extent; manpower, although we did not control manpower, the contractors as a control subject; and also to have a special responsibility for providing the facilities, the contractor facilities - that was part of the resource package.

So, one group said where we were going, the other said

what it takes to get there, and the one in the middle was my review group, and they were essentially assigned the responsibility of telling how well we were doing getting from here to there. A very simple concept. We had a nice little trilogy there, as it were, a troika, of associated staff activity. In the process, we did at a point in time pick up some other jobs that nobody else wanted, really.

We did take up the technical function of communications as an assignment to one of my staff. We had the training responsibility.

Q: That was the involvement?

Mr. P.: Yes. So we had a communications man on my staff. And we had responsibility for ensuring that the Bureau of Supplies and Accounts had tooled up the supply supporting system to support us, so had given the Special Project office the responsibility to ensure that they were doing what had to be done to support the operations.

Q: How long did it take you to develop this whole set up?

Mr. P.: Oh, now you're asking me for a time.

Q: Time being a very important element in this whole project.

Mr. P.: Well, in a sense, we had a breathing spell in my end of this thing because of the Jupiter involvement. You know the story. We stayed around Engine Charley Wilson for almost a year to adapt the Jupiter missile to a ship-launch capability.

Bill Hasler and some of the major work that was going on there was to be done at Huntsville, Redstone Arsenal, and we had Bill Hasler down there trying to modify the Jupiter missile, make it fatter and shorter, so it might fit.

Q: This took up about the first half of 1956?

Mr. P.: Yes. During that first year there were a lot of ingenious approaches as to how you were going to launch this beast. The Jupiter missile was about as big as a pullman car full of liquid oxygen. If you funneled liquid into it you could set fire to it and it would have blown up a ship. The Navy was very concerned about that. You know the story, the technical story. They discovered a better way to get the specific impulse improved in solid propellants.

Q: Would you talk a little about Wilson's attitude towards this? Why did he insist upon this marriage of the two efforts?

Mr. P.: I can't speak knowledgeably, except in terms of the general feeling at the time. I'm sure you know the background. The Von Neuman Committee made three recommendations, there will be building an ICBM, there will be a Jupiter, and there will be something that will be taken to sea. They went all out on the Air Force. They had the top priority on that. I think it was the Atlas at the time.

The Army had been building a Jupiter missile under cover. They were not even supposed to be in the missile business, but it got uncovered, a 1,500-mile land-based missile, which you can't reach from any place in the U.S., but I guess they rationalized that in terms of we'll get some allies to let us shoot it from their places.

But when the possibility of using something on which there'd already been some money spent for a second purpose, Wilson just bought it as something that made sense to him. In the same way that McNamara tried to get the Air Force and the Navy to adopt the same airplane in the interests of so-called economy. The Navy had to go along with it because it didn't have enough confidence they could build a solid propellant. You know they just went through this horrible experience with this missile that went up and down again.

Q: The Regulus?

Mr. P.: No, the Regulus was air-breathing. It's launched from a submarine. This was a Serva, a modification of a B-2. But that's later on. They didn't have a solid propellant that would work, and then the research, you know the story about that. They found that if they out massive amounts of powdered aluminum into the mix, it gave it the PSI they needed, and that opened up a whole new ball game. At the same time, you know the other story of how the Atomic Energy Commission reported a nuclear warhead that could be smaller so that the solid propellant could lift this warhead and carry it far enough. Those two things came together about - I would guess it was in the first year.

Q: It's interesting that that development on the part of the Atomic Energy Commission was not immediately known by the Navy. It came by way of Woods Hole.

Mr. P.: That's right, just sort of slipped in the back door.

Q: And Red Ramage was the message-carrier.

Mr. P.: I think he was, yes.

Raborn used to make speeches, some of them were rather good, on the subject of this business of being exposed. The responsibility of the management as to being exposed, having that radar tower to new knowledge, not just receiving it, but you'd go out and track these things, always looking for the implications on what we were working on. But that one did come by accident. We hadn't organized our radar system at that time to technology in all its various fields. That was an awfully important input to the success of the program because people were encouraged to be sensitive to new possibilities. If you get wired in on the right circuitry, it's amazing how much intelligence moves along informal lines by word of mouth. He motivated people to want to do these things - wanting to find out about new ideas and knowing that they would be received as a part of the communications system, which was far more important, in a sense, than any other procedures that we developed there. It was a human system that worked, as human system work in any if you tune them up properly. Get people, as people, interested.

You asked how long it took. Well, that first year, of course, we were struggling, trying to establish relationships all across the board up to the Bureau of the Budget. In that area of activity we were pretty busy.

Q: This is how you were utilizing that breather period?

Mr. P.: Yes. Well, we were on   always looking for money, trying to persuade people that even Jupiter would work, although we didn't like it. There was a sort of a reluctant participation doing something that had to be done, although I don't think there was anybody in   who really believed it would work. Deke Ela, you ought to hear him talk, he was an absolutely marvelous fellow.

Q: Who?

Mr. P.: Deke Ela. He's probably probably an admiral now. He had the launcher and the launching system, and carried us through those early days very colorfully. He was one of the real strong men on the technical side. He came up in a matter of days with the most ingenious launching devices to kick this

Jupiter missile out of the way so it wouldn't blow up the ship. A real Rube Goldberg, and he continued - I don't know where he is now. He's out of the Navy, but he's somewhere around. I really shouldn't say this because I don't know how much Frank did on fire control and Lou Shock did on the navigation center, but Deke Ela was an improvisor, he was the guy who improvised the polyp system by using some derricks out at Mare Island that were used to pull gun turrets off. He designed a system for catching a missile as it came out of the water. He designed the sky hook things. All these nice phrases, but they were just improvisations, you see and, in a sense, Deke Ela probably responded to something that I attribute to Levering Smith, one of the most positive statements of Levering Smith when he said we haven't got million-dollar bills to throw at our problems, which is good, now we have to think about them. Of course, this was a reference to some extent to the fact that at that time the Air Force had half of the defense budget, 20 billion dollars. I think the Navy had about 12 and the Army had 8. So we were constantly being exposed to this million-dollar confetti approach to weapon development. Levering took that and made it a positive thing - we haven't got enough money to just throw money away and, as a result, we got this creative, adaptive research, as it were.

Q: Duress makes it necessary!

Mr. P.: Yes, and people instead of standing around wringing their hands - oh, if we could only get another 50 or 56 million dollars, think of what we could do, they just sort of accepted it and said, well, let's work our way around this. I think probably that came from or as a result of of the experience   . We had to learn how to adapt things with limitations which should be the   of the military anyway. By definition, military training places great emphasis on the conservation of resources. Before you take a hill with ten men or twenty men you decide whether the hill is worth risking the ten men to do it with. So it's all in the doctrine of a military man, but they sometimes don't carry that over to money as they should. It should be basic   taught at Annapolis because they've got so much to work with. There is an awful lot of bad feeling, misunderstanding, suspicion, and so on, that they would build more strongly than I think they have on that one quality which a military man has and is unique to him, the conservation of resources, do the job with the least amount of resources you have to use because the resources of a military situation cost lives. I could carry that over into some other of whether they have any money a lot of the controls that have been set up and were no longer necessary. Basic suspicion, I think, was off the track.

Yes, the first year was that, but in the meantime the contractor that we had with us in BuOrd was Chrysler Corporation.

They were the prime contractors on the Jupiter missile, so our association was rather directly with them, as we tried to tie what they were doing into what we wanted the Army to do for us in modifying the Jupiter. And we spent a little time out at Chrysler, on the assumption that it was a blue-ribbon company quite successful in the automobile business and must have some very sophisticated men for tools and so on, and we even gave them a contract to help us set up a management information system. This was before I joined, although if I had been there I wouldn't have done that because we were looking for consulting.

We spent a little time out there and we found they may have known how to put fenders on Chryslers and Dodges and so on, but they didn't know how to manage a complicated operation that could not be mechanically automated. I mean it's one thing to set up an assembly line but it's another thing to set up an information system that controls something that's not physical like an assembly line.

So, while they got a contract for doing something that I   Raborn for doing, maybe physically designing what's called a management center room, I don't think that we kept them on our contract for more than a couple of months because it became obvious that they were building a cardboard and paste-pot jungle. Everything was associated with big cards visible at great distances, hundreds of little girls pasting things on these cards, which was their approach to visualizing the information that management needed, and we actually designed a room to accommodate all this cardboard before we finally got ahold of the subject and said this is ridiculous. It isn't going to satisfy our needs at all. It's too cumbersome.

Adm. C.: That, I think, is why they were ultimately dropped from the whole project.

Mr. P.: Yes. Well of course, when we got off Jupiter, they got off anyway, but we got them off their involvement with our management system before we got off the Jupiter contract.

Q: This is beside the point, but, in industry at that time, were there such management systems inexistence?

Mr. P.: I didn't plumb that one. J. B. could help on that one. I understand that Red Raborn and Ed Mernone do go visiting around in various laboratories and various places trying to find out what their systems were for managing research and development projects. All I get out of it is the answer that nobody had anything that the people who were running it had any confidence in, and there was nothing there that apparently appealed to   .

Adm. C.: I think, as near as I can recall, that they actually ran into a variety of very rudimentary systems, and I don't think anybody thought any of them were any better than the back of an envelope.

Q: The day for such systems had not yet arrived!

Adm. C.: They just had not, but there certainly was a recognition of the need because people were trying to set up systems, but they didn't have one, as I recall.

Mr. P.: That's the way it comes through. It was written about at the time. Red kept saying he looked around out when he talked to the people who were running these systems that they were 50 percent good, but still in his judgment and my judgment and so on if we didn't have enough time we took some more time. Time was probably the most critical factor that we had to work with. It was even more critical than money..

Adm. C.: I think perhaps the essential element that was missing in any of these rudimentary systems was the concept of critical path, which is what you introduced.

Mr. P.: That was part of it.

Adm. C.: Without that, it doesn't do you an awful lot of good to know that, well, this one is coming along fine and it's going to be ahead, this element down here is coming along slowly and it isn't going to quite make it - how do you pull that stuff together. You've got to have some way to determine what these critical paths are, so that you know instinctively that you've got a problem somewhere. You know how to fix it. How do you go about fixing it?

This, I think, was really the essence of your system.

Mr. P.: Yes, but I would use a different word. The word I'm going to use existed before we went to PERT and the critical path technique. The word I'm going to use is context. I started off by saying when you created a program and you defined its elements, the problem that we had was identifying where things related one to another, and to keep this in constant focus not only for the purpose of what J.B.'s talking about where if something fell down you sensed its impact on some other part of the program, but again for this very important motivational value, it permitted people to see how even their little bit of a job fitted into something that was a lot, lot bigger, so they would do it.

Q: Was that immediately apparent?

Mr. P.: I think I can say that it was because it had been so strong in my own management philosophy, and before we went to PERT - remember, we had those program management plans?

Adm. C.: Yes.

Mr. P.: We laid out a system that was invented in-house - we went outside for some consulting contracts on the PERT system, but before then we laid out individual plans which we set up - well, I could give you a drawing of them - and we said, now, ~~would~~ we want to be able to describe what we're doing in a way that will give answers to what it is, why it is, when it is required, how you're going to do it, and who's going to do it, and we devised it and designed a little form. We wanted to fit these plans into a planning system, so that from a big plan we'd break into subplans and finally get down to a contractor level and, at any one point in time, with a coding system, you could find out what any piece or any individual plan could be related to the plans that it supported or were supported by. And it's very, very good concept, but I'd hadn't seen at that time anything quite comparable to it.

Now, PERT grew out of that system because it became a little bit too awkward to handle in the time that we had to process these little charts. We used paper worksheets in which the what was here, the components of the big fleet ballistic missile system, and we identified four components: hardware, people, and the facilities. And then we had another column along the side that described

Anyway, the format is not too important. It was the answer that we provided that was important. This was called the Program Management Plan. We used big worksheets and then reduced them to the size that would fit into a folder, and the what was here, the components of the what were here - if the what was a missile system, the components might be the warhead, the motor, and the generators, and so on. Over here, on this part of the chart, we had time, depending on what time we were alloted - it could be three years or it could be two months. And then we described, now that's the what, subdivided, and then we said the how. We specifically limited this sheet of paper to 25 milestones: these things will have to be done in order to accomplish - and we put the why over here - so that over here we had a little thing like that. This was chronological, so when I put it on that kind of an axis my line goes like so.

We'd put in as many why's as we needed. I want to do these five things in order to produce this. Do these five things in order to have our first test, for example. Do the next four things in order to have our first launching. So, that's the why over here and that's the what, and the who was very important. We divided the who was responsible for doing this thing in terms of "directly responsible," "supporting," and "monitoring." "Monitoring" was a positive word. It didn't mean just passively waiting for somebody to tell you. It meant going out and finding out about it.

So, for every one of these milestones, there was an identification as to who was responsible for our accomplishing the milestone and in what way he was responsible. This might be an SP code, or it might be a contractor, or it might be a university, or a laboratory, or something. Each of these had a number. The top one was No. 1, the next number was in the 10 series, and then it went on down to about the fourth tier, which meant that we not only had a system - Raborn wrote a very important memorandum that set this whole thing up at one time, which I reference in the paper I gave you, in which he was asking the people who were making proposals to him to make their proposals in the terms of this, so he could see what they were talking about, how what they were doing related to the other things, what their milestones were, and their purposes for accomplishing these things.

Q: Did they respond readily to that?

Mr. P.: Oh, yes. This was accepted even with greater ease than some of the original PERT stuff was, because this was real stuff. We then gave these to the contractors. These became the terms on which our contract reporting system was based, and you could handle highly classified information because all they would have to do is to cite the number and the milestone on a teleform, "No. 27, yes," or "No go," you see. It's the simplest kind of code. Unless you've got the document, you wouldn't know what was going on.

The contractors were obviously involved in preparing these things. They had to accept these milestones.

Then we had one that I think was probably one of your innovations, J.B., the Progress Officers, either you or Red Raborn. But as part of the second or third part of my staff, the U group, they assigned some bright young officers - they were probably one- or two-year enlistees or somethey, they were ensigns and a few JGs - they were assigned to my staff but they had two hats. They were also assigned to each of the technical divisions. It was their job to ensure that if anything happened or didn't happen in their area, that they would communicate with the technical division about it. They would point out that this thing is happening in navigation, this thing relates to what is happening in the launching system. It was sort of a personalized communications system that we had. These only cost a penny when you got down to the point. I was rather proud of that. You could write these things up, type them up, put changes on the worksheet and take a picture of them, which cost a penny, and we had a communications system back to our contractor. And we also had the negative that we used to take the picture and it became a viewgraph, which you then put on a rear-view mirror or rear-view screen projector in our management center, so that all the conversations that took place - and I expect you've gone through the routine about how we ran those management meetings. It meant that the directors stood up and talked to their progress in these terms, and then in another set of terms, which I was even more pleased about.

We were not interested in building huge statistical sand piles of reports, which so commonly is the case, nor simple distillates of a lot of statistical data, so called parameter reporting at the top, which really doesn't mean anything. That has been so dehydrated.

Our reporting system was based on what we called "need to know," and that defined the terms in which we needed to know things. Things happened or they didn't happen. But even then, we didn't just that and those were thermometer charts, impressively so. We didn't want the technical directors, the directors of the technical divisions, to stand up and give us complicated reports on the data that they might have come into possession of. What Raborn wanted was their judgment of the significance of the data, and we reduced that to the simplest possible terms - "good shape," "minor weakness," "major weakness," "critical." And every week with some of them it was up and down. They were the terms in which responsible people talked to other people. On my poop sheet you notice that "good shape" meant, "Boss, everything that I was supposed to do this week or I hoped to do has been done. You might give me a few compliments on this thing." Or "minor weakness," something happened that I didn't want to happen, but I know what it is, I can correct it. Just want you to know about it. "Major weakness," something ahppened. I need help, I need more money, I need some additional assistance. "Critical" very simply "Boss, you need help. Better go and see the Secretary about this one."

I repeat, that was the response of people talking to

people in a responsible way, rather than just burying them with 200-page memoranda, which you can cover yourself in as many different ways as you like.

Q: But you can't always assimilate verbally?

Mr. P.: No, but the easiest way to conceal the truth is to write a 200-page report on it.

Q: Incidentally, were the compliments forthcoming when they were deserved?

Mr. P.: Oh, yes. That was part of, well, I started out with Raborn, but J.B. and   after. Yes, the credit lines helped. They were not only unsparing, but they were intelligent compliments. I think I can say this with some rather strong feeling. People were complimented on the things that they felt they should be complimented on, because what they were doing could be seen again in my favorite word "context." "You did a good job on that because it makes it now possible for some other thing," they weren't just generalized, "you did a good job" and that kind of thing. That was a byproduct, a spin-off value, motivational value from having created a complex.

Then,   PERT   show computer-based statistical massage of the data which was becoming too voluminous for us to identify in this manual approach and

Adm. C.: It was sort of like the progression in the Stock Exchange from hand-chalking to computerized control. There was just so much of it you couldn't do it by hand any more. We'd have had a roomful of people shuffling papers, probably not fast enough for anybody to get any good out of it.

Mr. P.: Well, that's that's a progression from what Chrysler did because they were enamored with these huge charts and a lot of paste pots. Then we went to that. They understood that in the Navy capability for massaging data yet bringing out the answer you were looking for, which again was "context" you see.

Q: And you were in an electronic age so you could do it and make use of it?

Mr. P.: Yes. We succeeded to a fairly new development. It came at the right time.

Mr. P.: Yes, the   for the Nautilus computer. Did you have it at Dahlgren?

Adm. C.: Oh, yes.

Mr. P.: What has happened to Llewellyn Thompson? Is he still living?

Adm. C.: I understand that he is alive. He's pretty ill and,

I think, pretty feeble. I'm not so sure whether his mind works all the time or not.

Mr. P.: Well, he is getting up in years, but he was a great strength to us in the working of the North computers. I was telling these GAM people who said "What's the simplest answer to what made Polaris go?" and I think if you have to have simple answers it's that it was a program in which people were not only permitted but encouraged and, in a sense, required to think together. That sounds kind of corny, but that's what happened. The environment was such that people thought together in a common objective and it cuts through an awful lot of emotional barriers that separate thought, thought.

Q: It was the initial need for money and also the time element which produced this squeeze that made you -

Mr. P.: Yes and nobody got excited about it. I'm not saying . I think he did. I don't know whether without that kind of exterior environment, sputnik scare, this grapefruit in the sky, and the missile gap, whether it would have come off or not. Obviously it could have worked in a wartime but This system worked without wartime control and without wartime motivation. The motivation was given to us in part and we built on it. All the presentations on the subject were motivational in purpose, whether they were in a parking lot at Lockheed or Aerojet or at one of our other contractors' plants, or whether with the wives sitting down on a Saturday afternoon listening to why their husbands never showed up for dinner, and so on.

There was an investment in motivation.

Q: But wasn't it true that there was an element of wartime motivation in terms of self-preservation? I mean this was a keynote in the preservation of the nation?

Adm. C.: It certainly was as far as we were concerned. I think essentially all of the people in the project were convinced that this was something that had to be done and had to be done expeditiously and it had to work. We were all convinced. In fact, whenever new people came on board, about the only instructions they got, they got education, but the only instruction they got was, "now, you've got to believe it."

Mr. P.: Of course, it was a very sexy program and maybe that's the main thing that was going for it. The sea is an emotional thing - ships at sea, and so on. The idea of concealment. It was a real sexy program because it was invulnerable, it stalked unknown - you could put all the PR words around it and yet you were telling the truth. A submarine can lie under the ice caps like a rattlesnake under a stone and so on! I mean we could get some good people who knew how to carpenter the right kind of words. This was something. It was the answer to our problems.

Adm. C.: We had some pretty high-grade wordsmithing in this

period.

Mr. P.: We sure did. Old Tom Watson, I see him quite often.

Q: Red Raborn acknowledged that his family background, the Bible belt, and the fact that he had preachers in the family, had some bearing on the way he conducted himself, going out on the circuit!

Mr. P.: He was on the circuit. It sounds kind of funny to say it, but I suppose some other people were, Ben Schreiver and so on, but he was a past master at it. The man is I'm not saying this critically but honestly, I heard people say, "I wish I knew what he said. I believe what he said, but I wish I understood what he was saying!"

Adm. C.: Conveyance was the thing, yes. I mean you knew he was saying something that you wanted to believe in and yet it was kind of hard to follow.

Q: Well, this is where he was saying that he was drawing on the gospel-preacher attitude of his forebears.

Adm. C.: And what he was selling was the idea that here's a man that I want to believe in and he was a very believable leader. His record will support that.

Q: Maybe this is an appropriate time to talk about the planned publicity for the whole program.

Mr. P.: Well, I must say it was through the grape vine in a sense and somebody sitting down let's do this.

Q: You use that term in your paper.

Mr. P.: Yes. Well, it was planned, in a sense, to be insistent on bringing as many people in to hear our story, to convert it as it were, as you could possibly get over there. This was a very important method of operating, as far as Raborn was concerned. paper around

He would rather persuade them that what we were doing was something they should identify. So part of this organization was to get a contracting officer here, even on the fringes of a program, saying, yes, I know what they're doing. I'm going to help them, even though I may be another trifling bit of help. That was more visual.

The other part of it and a very important part of it, we had to convince an awful lot of people that what we were saying was true because there were an awful lot of lies being talked around Washington, some of them based on ignorance, some on malice, if you want to get inter-service on this thing. And there were an awful lot of people who were just skeptical, inside the Navy, about whether this thing would ever work.

Adm. C.: Especially the ones who lost money in order to do it!

Mr. P.: Right.

Q: This was in the very early stages, wasn't it?

Adm. C.: Oh, no. And, of course, it never was funded over and above the Navy budget. A lot of people suspected and hoped that it would be, but it wasn't. Even though, after the first year, we had our own money in the budget, there isn't any doubt ~~that~~ but what the rest of the Navy lost in order to put money in Polaris, there just isn't any question about it.

Mr. P.: We tried the best, and of course the Navy had its own reasons, to refuse for a long time to even put the weapon system into the strategic weapon category. The Air Force said that's what it is, therefore we want it. But when we said, yes, that's what it is, give us part of your strategic warfare money, they said no. So we lost both ways, you see, for a period of time there. The Navy was parading this weapon system as something they were going to use to knock out the submarine pens, even though we knew right from the beginning that it was a strategic weapon. But there was a roles and mission argument taking place in the Pentagon at that time. -

Adm. C.: Which had some pretty poor

Mr. P.: Yes, they wanted to get hold of this program, youssee, and the Navy wasn't about to let the Air Force start running the fleet.

So part of the planed reputation of what we were doing was motivational, part of it was honestly educational, trying to educate our critics. This took many forms. It's easy to recite particular episodes. I'll tie this example to something   was talking about, namely the courage of Admiral Raborn. I see a very courageous man who set fire two when the first one fired on July 20th from the George Washington. It would have been so easy to just fire one and go back to port, but he took the chance the second one would work. That takes guts. But even before then, I give him full marks on this one, we were involved in a budgetary flap at a time when Congress was pressing for more votes for submarines and the Navy   money. I was there - maybe you know, no, this was after your time - Franke, the Secretary of the Navy, was trying to deal with them, "I'll give you the momey, but I won't give it to you for research and development. I'll give you the money long lead time on three more boats, so that we can go to Congress and say that we're putting three more boats into the program, instead of one."

Raborn said, "I don't want the damn boats. If I can't have the money for my research, there's no point in building the boats." He stood on that and part of his presentation that came out in his newsletter - we'd just put our PERT charts into   we used butcher paper and the biggest PERT chart   two walls, and a couple of sailors   to Creighton's office. We knew what the argument was going to be because Raborn turned down the   . So as soon as unfolded this PERT chart

Jim Wakelin was there and we stretched that butcher paper on two walls, it must have been at least 40 feet or more, all this diagram. It was legitimate. We were using it, but we'd had the wit to roll it up and bring it over. Well, this answered the question:

"Now, this, Mr. Secretary, is what it means to manage a research and development program. Now, tell me, where can I take my foolish dollars out

They were just buzz words, you know, research and development people sitting around on their ditty boxes wasting money, but when you laid it out in terms of a diagram - maybe it appealed to him because he was a plumber, like a plumber's diagram. And we got
We got some additional money

Q: He said, when I talked with him, that Raborn just wore him down, that he kept going back. That he'd say, hell, no, and the next day he'd be back with the same question, and finally he wore me down.

Mr. P.: I don't think I've ever told this and I don't know whether it's proper. You can delete it from the record if you want to. Raborn had Franke worried. I remember one day he called me, very quietly over the telephone he asked me to come on over there. What he was doing was trying to find out whether Raborn was telling the truth.

Q: He wanted corroboration!

Mr. P.: Yes. I was amused and told Red all about it.
          if he wants to develop an independent source of information, but I told Red.

But you could sort of sense the position of the Secretary because he was a pretty persuasive salesman.

Q: Your planned publicity was intended not only for the education of specific people and of Congress, but for the populace as a whole, was it not?

Mr. P.: Yes. We had two PR people. I say PR you were asking me my responsibilities, I got George Carter and Commander Moran. George Moran was just a real solid guy. There was a media story and they were our contacts because we had a very unusual story, it was classified in its detail but certainly not in its import   and we had to work on that rather carefully because at that time there was a missile gap and every time any kind of a rocket blew up at Canaveral, it made a newsworthy story, and we were popping some rockets down there, I think, the first four of them, the A-1, 2, 3, and 4, went up and then came down again, and that made a good story, so we had to bear the brunt of this kind of a missile failure, and what they couldn't see at Canaveral, the other services were very happy to fill in the details!

So we had that kind of a protective public relations program.

Q: I see, yes.

Mr. P.: Over and above that on the PR side - and here we adopted or began to think of film reports, which we needed - You know, a for our own pictures and ten thousand words and so on - we invested in a certain amount of documentary evidence of what was going on at the contractors and at the tests, but other things as well. These, of course, became available material for other uses. We checked them as reports from our contractors and then used them as reports to the people in the Pentagon and the people on the Hill, and some of them were very effective.

Of course, I think probably the biggest PR coup that we ran off, with, we got CBS Edward Murrow a half-hour documentary on it   or something like that   did the documentary on it, but that was a good show. It ran a whole hour

Pehrson - 44

They did one on the Army's profile of a missile. We got a commitment from them that no matter what happens to it, we're going to follow this all the way from Chrysler all the way through the   , even if it blows up.

Q: And they used it?

Mr. P.: They used it.

Adm. C.: You know, the Army started off with one they called Redstone, which was about a 400-mile bird, or something like that, maybe less. Actually, for one as primitive as that, it was a pretty darned good bird, pretty reliable.

Mr. P.: Yes, I was trying to remember. It was the Vanguard. The Vanguard was a fiasco. Nobody thought Polaris with that history wasn't going to follow the same pattern.

Q: How did Watson contribute with his graphics and his ability at presentations in this publicity area?

Mr. P.: Well, just about the way you described it. Have you met him at all? Old Tom Watson?

Q: I interviewed him.

Mr. P.: Oh, did you? He had a knack for taking almost any subject, I don't care how dull it might be, and making it graphically interesting and meaningful. I'm somewhat prejudiced in my enthusiasm for him because Tom Watson - I met him on this program, he'd written a book, a sort of in-house Navy lecture series for the then CNO, I think it was Carney. I'd met him there and so I told Raborn, "Look, this man has written a book on this subject. He's got the recipe." He said, "I don't want the book, I want the author. We've got to get him associated with us."

I've had an association with him all the years since. I've worked with him in   he went to Greece with me and he had some of my contracts. I don't know any subject which he cannot make interesting and meaningful by just looking at some of the data and then working out a set of photographic relationships that will highlight it.

Adm. C.: In addition to an encyclopedic knowledge of the various techniques that are successful, that snag your attention and keep it - in addition to that, he has a very unusual sense of what it is that you're trying to do. The combination is terrific. This is what he gave us. He gave us real expertise in putting a slide show together and the actual construction of individual slides. He was just awfully good at it.

Mr. P.: I'm glad you brought that up. He's not just a consultant. He's a fellow who'll work till three o'clock in the morning on a particular layout. He comes out of an advertising background. He was with J. Walter Thompson, which was described to me once by Elmo Roper,   , as probably one of the four top influences in American advertising.

Adm. C.: Really, top four?

In addition to the knowledge, he just has an instinctive feel for what's good.

Mr. P.: Oh, yes, he's been operating for the Navy for many, many years. Who was CinCPac?

Adm. C.: Jack McCain.

Mr. P.: Yes, he worked with Jack McCain when Jack first started his seapower speeches.

Q: He was selling sea power, yes.

Adm. C.: The five oceans.

Q: And Hank Miller was with him, then.

Mr. P.: It goes back years and years. But, over and above the actual work he did on graphics, he had a great deal of influence on our people in terms of teaching them how to present ideas. He did it beautifully on presentational ideas, the do's and the don'ts.

Adm. C.: He was a professor for the staff in addition to the individual work he did. One of the things I learned from him which I've always remembered and which I've attempted to use, or did when I was in the business of speaking to people at presentations or personal appearances or whatever, was don't give anybody a chance to ask you a question. Answer his question before he asks it.

Secondly, don't ever present anything to anybody which is easily open to argument, which is an automatic argument, because it'll come out and then you're off on some hare-brained offshoot argument. You've lost him as an audience, you've lost your own train of thought, and you're dead.

Q: And often emotion -

Adm. C.: Especially emotion, avoid that at all costs.

Mr. P.: In the presentational ideas there's a lot of psychology involved. Take any group of people, whether it's a group of military people or the chairman of the board - a board meeting or something - there are going to be some people for you and some people are against you, no matter what you say. Forget about the first and the second   you give them a little argument so they can add to their own reportery. Always work on the don'ts at any time when the guy's

Q: Who's convinced, yes. How did Jack Dunlop fit into your scheme of things?

Mr. P.: Well, Dunlop of course was - have you talked to him, too?

Q: Yes.

Mr. P.: Well, then, you know his strength at that time, as he was brought into our program, was so-called human engineering. I don't know how Raborn used him other than that, but he had a continuing   . He was just another discipline, another professional, viewpoint that was being brought to bear on the engineering decisions that were taking place all over, but also in the - I'm not the best qualified to comment on this sort of thing, but I would say on the first part as an indirect, OK, so you're building a missile and you've got this piece in there that's got to be turned off or you've got to replace it, let's be damned sure there's a hole inside the missile long enough for to get in. That's real gutsy engineering, for the fact that at some point in time a man has to do something to this piece of stuff.

But I think it's fairly sophisticated work in terms of the control, the subject of control layouts, because his professional field is in measuring eye impacts. They've got probably the best talent up there on the impact of color, peripheral vision, what one can see and what one can't see, how to make a dial, how do you really put in relation to man, who's in an operational thing.

The admiral always saw Jack was around. He was at most of the meetings.

Q: He was on that board, wasn't he, of advisors?

Pehrson - 49

Mr. P.: The Steering Task Group? No.

Q: No, the Steering Group.

Mr. P.: He could have been, I don't remember.

Adm. C.: I don't remember seeing him around very much at the time I was there because we actually hadn't gotten to the human engineering part. We didn't have any hardware yet.

Q: The human engineering was concerned with industry, wasn't it?

Adm. C.: Yes, and that was a little bit after I was there.

Mr. P.: Just how long were you there. Two years?

Adm. C.: I left in January of 1958.

Mr. P.: That may have been after he came along. He got rather involved -

Adm. C.: He may have been on contract when I was there, but I don't remember that there was an awful lot for him to do until later.

Mr. P.: I don't know exactly what the details around his but I know Levering had a   that somebody gave him for design engineer who'd been working on some kind of a gadget and surrounging him with half a dozen other people with various names, safety engineer, human engineer, controlling quality engineer. They were all kibitzing on these poor guys trying to design something.

Adm. C.: I say I don't know how you did it because we did have special attention given to quality control. We had to rewrite the book on that one, apparently. There obviously were safety considerations, and the human engineering side, but I don't remember any real knock-down-drag-out on the subject. The talents were brought in and apparently in the right way so that their influence was felt.

Q: Who was responsible for -- I suppose the term is "fragmentation" in industry and the segregation of the Polaris from the rest of the operations?

Adm. C.: I think that was probably Raborn more than anyone else. I think he simply issued an edict to each one of the contractors, "You will have a Polaris division and it will be separate from the rest so that it doesn't get contaminated doesn't get involved, and the people that work on Polaris are going to work on Polaris. I don't want to find any of them any place else in the plant. This is just the way it's going to be, fellows." And that's the way it was.

I think it was Raborn.

Mr. P.: I thought you were asking how they selected Lockheed and General Electric which I don't know. That question came up this morning over at the GAO. I don't know whether they were a kind of   selection and everybody and their brothers hanging on.

Adm. C.: I know how it was done.

Mr. P.: Maybe it was Raborn and you who said, oh, Aerojet, Mr. Thiokel and so on, let's go there.

Adm. C.: No. I think there were about five of us on the board at the time, and we went back one evening after dinner, sat down in front of a blackboard, and we drew a matrix of what we considered to be, and this was strictly a matter of judgment, the strength and the weaknesses of the various candidates.

Mr. P.: Oh, I didn't know this. It's very interesting.

Adm. C.: You had Chrysler, you had Lockheed, you had GE, and there probably were a couple more, but I don't remember. We put down all these things. It was purely judgment. Nobody had anything to prove -

Q: The only thing you had anything on was Chrysler!

Adm. C.: Yes, that's right. We just stared at that for a while and finally we started adding up pluses and minuses, and they were not very distinctive either. Finally, we sort of all said, yes, let's go with Lockheed!

Pehrson - 52

Mr. P.: Was Firestone in the picture at that time?

Adm. C.: Of course, that would have been second tier.

Q: That's Thiokel Chemical, isn't it?

Adm. C.: Yes. They would have been candidates for the motor. As I remember, Lockheed chose   and their choice was agreed to by SP.

Mr. P.: I know there was some jurisdictional floundering around there between the Lockheed and the Aerojet   . Somebody had to decide just how they related to one another.

Adm. C.: One of the things that came up for discussion many times, over a long period, was the matter of fees. These people were all getting a percentage and the question was raised why does Lockheed give their own fee, then they'd also give a fee on the money that goes to Aerojet, because Lockheed doesn't actually do anything for that money.

Q: Double taxation! See on fee.

Adm. C.: It was fee on fee, that's right. A lot of people kept asking these questions, and I thought it was a very good question but, within the procurement regulations, within the law, this is OK. You can't take it away from them! This was discussed frequently.

Lockheed's choice of Aerojet I think was pretty much based on early results with big motors of high specific impulse.

Mr. P.: Well, they were jeto –

Adm. C.: They started with that, that's correct. So they got the motor contract.

Q: Some of the choices were very obvious ones, weren't they, like when you got on down to the building of the submarine itself. Electric Boat was an obvious one.

Adm. C.: EB was an obvious choice for a starter.

Mr. P.: Yes, of course. No one else   I know GE

Adm. C.: GE was logical for fire control, yes, and I think Westinghouse was quite logical for the launching gear. They had been building very large pieces of machinery for quite a long time.

Did you ever go to that old Joshua Handy plant that Westinghouse bought out there? It was made out of redwood, a huge thing.

Mr. P.:

Adm. C.: Yes, a lot of the choices were pretty logical. To get back to the choice of Lockheed, you could never put that on an adding machine anywhere and make it stand up. It was just a matter of judgment.

Mr. P.: Probably the most skeptical one was on the navigation side. I had the impression that old Lou Shock was sort of like running around like a housewife in a super market shopping. He didn't know why either a startracker or a moontracker from from   and a pitometer from   and SINS from here and Lord knows what all. Sort of jury-rigging from

Adm. C.: There wasn't any one contractor for navigation. Today, if we had it to do over we wouldn't have permitted that to happen, but it worked out.

Mr. P.: Sperry came through, they could pretty much the firing element.

Adm. C.: They came on top of it later and took charge of it.

Mr. P.: He was doing it, incidentally. He had a special job. He ended up with a couple of boats, the Mariner and the Observation Island   I say they "ended up with them" because they started work on those to put Jupiter on and fire it. Jupiter had to have big boats, so they used them as navigation test ships which, in a sense, they improvised. But I guess Lou had to find something to put on his boats even before the rest of the system had made any progress.

Adm. C.: Lou funded some very valuable developmental that never would have been done if it hadn't been done for Polaris.

Mr. P.: The electrostatic SINS? Did that ever get off the ground?

Adm. C.: The electrostatic gyro did get off the ground, yes, and he funded a lot of developmental work in radio star trackers. I don't know whether he did much in optical star tracking or not. Some, I guess. And something a little more exotic, he funded some very important developmental work in gravity-measuring devices, particularly ones that could be used in a surface ship rather than in a submarine, because the original ones you had to take into a submarine because it was so sensitive to ship's motion. It was a very interesting mess of stuff!

Q: In this paper that you prepared for the Senate, Mr. Pehrson, you made various points in the way of a summary. Do you want to talk about some of them? I think they're very interesting indeed.

Mr. P.: What were they?

Q: Well, the influence of the whole program on organization, program management.

Mr. P.: Yes. I'm afraid it hasn't had as much influence as I think it should have. Of course, I've entered the caveat before and I'll do it again that I may be somewhat prejudiced in my view as to the influence that really did take place.

But I would like to think that the example of the Special Project's approach to managing a program had a considerable influence on people like, say, Hitch, for example, and McNamara when he became Secretary of Defense. I can't say this, but they had arrived at the same conclusion themselves when they started thinking at that level in terms of strategic programs or values and tactical weapons systems and so on. They ascribed weapon systems to some military purpose. I'm not close enough to what has happened in the last fourteen years to know whether what started off to be what I thought was a very good decision deteriorated. I rather suspect it deteriorated for one very simple reason. I agreed with their centralizing at that level, the decisions about the value of a program, whether it was a strategic program and so on, because they got the subject in the right arena. So the centralizers were the "why" answers, and it was needed because there's an awful lot of fighting between the services as to who's going to do this and that.

Then the trouble was he also centralized the "how" answers, instead of providing from that level the approvals of programs and then letting the departments or bureaus or whoever giving them the job of doing it. He gathered around himself hundreds or thousands of deputized people who reviewed and analyzed the hell out of everything and started prescribing as to how things should be done in procurement, regulation, and all the rest of it. And that is the one function that should not be centralized   .

So I say the one influence went up and had a good result on centralizing programs and getting attention to program decisions that   . I don't even object to cost-benefits analysis, if properly handled. I think it got very badly handled under people like   and so on. But the concept is right, and there was a value judgment made as to what is the value of success in doing this from a military standpoint. So that was good.

I'm still talking about the argument that efforts can be brought together and defined in terms of a program.

I left SP quite deliberately to go over to the re-organized Bureau of Ordnance and Ships and BuWeps, because frankly I wanted to. xxxxxxxx And I'm sorry about that because it kind of left the SP people in a hole.

Q: When did you leave the SP?

Mr. P.: In about 1961, wasn't it? No, it was in 1960. It was right after they'd fire those two shots. Because I wanted to see whether some of the ideas that we had over there would work in a larger context, and we reorganized under P. D. Stroop and Schoech the Bureau of Weapons into a kind of an over-all program type of organization. We set up under Tommy Booth. Remember Tommy Booth?

Adm. C.: Yes, oh, yes.

Mr. P.: Well, Tommy Booth had the planning function. I was assistant director for budgets and so on. But we divided all the activities of BuWeps into certain program areas, like submarine warfare was a program. Everything we were doing was put into this program director's hands - air defense was another one. We ended up with about six of them, including one for space under that delightful Irishman.

Tommy Booth was No. 3 man in the organization. Admiral Stroop and Bill Schoech and Tommy Booth. He was the planning director and then he had these other program directors as part of his staff, and I was also a part of this staff on the side.

We went to work. We procedurized this thing. The only trouble was - and I'll never forgive him for doing it - they put captains and commanders in charge of the programs, and they left the admirals in charge of research and development and procurement and maintenance and so on. You knew who saluted who with that kind of a situation. The main point I keep making is that military judgment can be wrapped up in the seniority of an officer is what is required for program decisions, then the top admirals should have been in those program spots and let the civilians and lesser military people run these functions of procurement and so on. There's no military judgment involved, it's the judgment of intelligent people. But they didn't do it and it sort of fell apart.

I left to some extent   in industry and they tore it all apart. because after I left them they took the whole structure apart, brought in a rear admital, I guess, into my job and he threw it apart and went back to becoming comptroller of BuWeps because he understood money. I don't remember those names so I'm not talking about a person.

About that same time the Army got interested in some of the principles of the Polaris and some of the organizational structure of BuWeps, so I went down and helped them organize the Army Material Command - I say "helped them," I gave them a couple of lectures. What they were doing was copying BuWeps' pattern of organization. Then BuWeps turned around, after they'd taken the thing apart, looked at the Army and said "that looks good"! So they set up a Navy Material Command which apparently was patterned after the Army Material Command.

You talk about chasing your tail around! That was nothing. It's crazy to have cheap opinion, but I think probably that thing could have worked if we'd gotten the admirals in the right spots.

Q: They can be very useful these admirals, can't they!

Mr. P.: Well, they were being used as for their military wisdom in terms of making decisions about the programs for defense, the missile programs, and so on. Captain McKee, for example - what ever happened to him?

Adm. C.: He lives out in California now.

Mr. P.: He was a missile man for years and years and years.

Adm. C.: Yes, that's right.

Mr. P.: He was probably the senior program man we had.

Adm. C.: I forget who he went with. He's with some firm out in California.

Q: Another point that I think you might talk to is the new patterns of Adventure in Partnership, the new kind of relationship between government, industry, and universities, and so on.

Mr. P.: Well, I like the title. We used it in   and put together a book. It was financed by half a dozen big people. We got the contractors together and you put them together - you ought to ask him to show you a copy, if you have contact with him. We thought of it as an adventure in partnership   title and in our conversation. Unfortunately, that kind of a relationship became known as the military-industrial complex, which is a dirty word.

But, very encouragingly, my discussions with the GAO this morning and a copy of a report which they are writing for Congress is based on the study of eleven weapon systems cases, comes out very strongly for recognition of the arms-length dealing to have the   relationship just doesn't work.

Pehrson - 61

So maybe fifteen years later they'll finally get around to realizing that if you want to manage change you've got to hire people in the grade or situation where the right people can think objective, and no matter how thick they like their procurement manuals, how many advisory review boards, and supervisory staff they throw into the picture, until they get the contractor accepted as an honorable person to create the environment which he can share with you, in a common interest, you are not going to solve the kind of problems we've had with the C-5A and all the rest of it.. That was horrible, where give me a good contract and I'll make it for fun. He won't make it for fun because the nature of the subject has change, and there are problems creating an environment in which change might be intelligently handled without being contractually policed. And that's what started this thing here.

It was an adventure in partnership for the Steering Task Group, and it a lot of other things.

I don't know whether J.B. feels as strongly about this point as I do, but there were a lot of people that were brought into the SP office - not a lot of people, I don't think we ever had over 250 people - but they came from technical billets, both in uniform and as civilians. They came out of BuOrd and BuWeps and BuShips and BuAir, but where they'd been sitting at technical desks, making technical decisions. If I'm overstating what I want to say, please correct me. But I know

I made a strong point with Raborn that we are not set up in business here to invent things - that's not what we're here for. I think they actually had to throw some drawing boards out. There was a tendency for people who knew launching devices to say, I'm going to design a launching device, and use their authority to impose their design on a contractor, whereas the rationale of the approach that we were trying to create was "you will authenticate the process to design, you can offer your opinions on the subject, you cannot impose your opinions under the authority of having the money or the selection. We've got other means of doing it."

Now, was that honored more in the breach than in the observance?

Adm. C.: No. No, I think that's a correct statement. I said much the same thing. From the beginning, the intent of the Special Project office was to be overseers and decision-makers in the Washington arena, and I think the office continued to be pretty successful in that view.

Levering, of course, is a rather particular case. He is eminently capable of offering a technical fix for something that won't work, just because he knows so much about it. I think perhaps he's a special case.

Mr. P.: Yes. Well, remember Deke Ela designed that launching system and put on for the Jupiter missile. He was very create at engineering, but that's a basic thing and I think that's rather an important one. Otherwise, you get a duplicated staff and continual arguments about it. Of course, if your contractors have not performed that's all that happened.

Adm. C.: I believe, Gordon, that somebody told me one time the top numerical strength in the SP office in Washington was somewhere between 400 and 450, which, for the job being done, is very small.

Q: Incredible!

You spoke about the program as being an example of one that was carried out with time and performance objectives. How does that differ from any other approach?

Mr. P.: Well, time, of course - all programs have performance objectives, but I don't know of any program, other than in actual wartime, in which the factor of time had such a real value. This required Raborn constantly - there has to be a trade-off in idea against its time significance, can you do it this good in this time? Ok, we'll buy it. If I give you six months more, you can do so much better, but I want it six months earlier, so I'll take the lesser one.

Q: Sort of a grand-daddy of a crash program, wasn't it?

Mr. P.: Yes. There were people who used to be rather cynical about that.

Adm. C.: I think the reason for that can possibly be stated this way. For the first time, we had in our hands a program which was associated with the survival of the country. That's why time was so important.

Mr. P.: Well, it really was, and that was one of the sexier things. We'd say if we can do this we take this much time off, and that's why all the attention to our schedules and so on. That's why, for example, we made out this PERT system. We had a choice of trying to vector in on cost, performance, or time. We took time, and time is a control variable in the PERT system. It was extended to include cost later. They never reached for performance.

Q: But the primary was time?

Mr. P.: Was time, yes.

Adm. C.: Performance was allowed to become evolutionary. We had A-1, A-2, A-3, and then Poseidon.

Q: And when you succeeded in diminishing the time element from, what was it originally, ten years, why, this was a great fillip to the whole thing, wasn't it?

Adm. C.: Yes, an encouragement. Nine to four was the amount of cut, wasn't it?

Mr. P.: Well, you fired in 1960. When did you leave? Forgetting about Jupiter, we didn't do anything on the Polaris until a year after we got -

Adm. C.: Well, we had a certain amount of - we had a going organization which we didn't have to change.

We started in 1956 and shot in 1960, so we shot in four years, and the original guess had been nine. These were the successive accelerations.

Mr. P.: The major technical difference that was written up at the time, I suppose it still applies, (a) there was concurrent design. We worked on the launcher at the same time, we didn't wait for the missile, so there was concurrency. But there was also extrapolation of the state of the art do your thinking, if possible, in this time to reach this point. They were not always successful with the navigation side

Adm. C.: If I may interrupt for just a minute, associated with that was if we'd only get partway there, it'll work.

Mr. P.: Yes.

Q: Now is this a kind of an inversion of what Arleigh Burke told me, that there was a cut-off - ?

Adm. C.: That was separate. That was always in the background. If you came up to the fall-off-the-cliff point, obviously you don't pursue it. But none of us in the project ever thought that was going to happen.

Q: He intimated that at one point you had apparently reached the –

Mr. P.: That was when the A-1   . There was concern about it. There was a control problem on that that.

Adm. C.: I don't think you'd ever get Levering to admit that he thought it was going to fall off the cliff.

Q: Well, I thank you both.

DECLARATION OF TRUST

The undersigned does hereby appoint and designate as his (her) Trustee herein, the Secretary-Treasurer and Publisher of the United States Naval Institute to perform and discharge the following duties, powers, and privileges in connection with the possession and use of a certain taped interview between the undersigned and the Oral History Department of the United States Naval Institute.

1. Classification of Transcript.

(✓)a. If classified OPEN, the transcript(s) may be read or the recording(s) audited by the qualified personnel upon presentation of proper credentials, as determined by the Secretary-Treasurer of the U. S. Naval Institute.

( )b. If classified PERMISSION REQUIRED TO CITE OR QUOTE, the user will be required to obtain permission in writing from the interviewee prior to quoting or citing from either the transcript(s) or the recording(s).

( )c. If classified PERMISSION REQUIRED, permission must be obtained in writing from the interviewee before the transcribed interview(s) can be examined or the tape recording(s) audited.

( )d. If classified CLOSED, the transcribed interview(s) and the tape recording(s) will be sealed until a time specified by the interviewee. This may be until the death of the interviewee or for any specified number of years.

2. It is expressly understood that in giving this authorization, I am in no way precluded from placing such restrictions as I may desire upon use of the interview at any time during my lifetime, nor does this authorization in any way affect my rights to the copyright of my literary expressions that may be contained in the interview.

Witness my hand and seal this 7th day of May 1973.

I hereby accept and consent to the foregoing Declaration of Trust and the powers therein conferred upon me as Trustee:

Interview with Mr. Clement Hayes Watson

Place: His residence in West Redding, Connecticut

Date: Friday morning, 17 Nove,ber 1972

Subject: Polaris Program

By: John T. Mason, Jr.

Q: It's a great pleasure to meet you. I've been looking forward to this interview and looking forward to your account of your contribution to the development of the Polaris.

Would you begin, Sir, by telling me just in capsule form something about your public relations background and your Navy connection?

Mr. W.: The public relations background is roughly 28 years with the J. Walter Thompson Company, in which company I had a variety of jobs none of which was specifically public relations, but they involved originally art direction, then copy writing, and then I became a group head and was made head of the trade and industrial department and sent to open up one of our new offices on the continent which happened to be in Berlin. On my return from Berlin I was head of the radio department for a while, and then assumed the job of an account representative and vice president, which were almost synonymous in the advertising business, and handled a group of national accounts until I left the company in 1952 to become a consultant in a specialized field. And the specialized field was the outgrowth of a rather unusual combination of experience, because I started out as an art director and then became a copy writer, and then was connected very closely with the selling of the company and had some somewhat unorthodox ideas of how you should visualize material the way you would visualize an advertisement to project your story clearly and simply and attractively. That was rather unusual because, generally speaking, charts haven't changed in the last fifty years. So I started to develop a set of visual techniques which are quite unique, as far as I know, and ran this presentation activity at Thompson along with my other things. I had a group of youngsters whom I trained in these methods, and finally found that I was working 365 days a year trying to handle my accounts and develop this presentation business, which was now being drawn on by all the company's offices and by many of their clients.

So, when I had finished an assignment running our Latin American activities in 1952 I left the company and became an independent consultant in the field of presentation. I had done some of that work while I was on active duty in World War II, beginning as somewhat of a disciple of Lewis Strauss, and then developed for Lewis Strauss and Admiral Blandy presentations which were delivered to congressional groups, first, in matters of ordnance, and then later, to Mr. Forrestal dealing with the financial set-up of the Navy, and eventually I was one of three officers to develop the presentation made to Mr. Truman when he took office to acquaint him with the naval war and the plans for the future of the naval war.

In all of those assignments the job was to take a fairly complex problem and shake it into its fundamentals and express it in an understandable way to a person who was not a professional in that field. In fact, it has been bruited about the Pentagon that if Watson can understand a subject any fool can understand the subject. So my job was usually a matter of elimination and simplification and not getting into technical details.

Q: A terribly essential function, I would think.

Mr. W.: Well, take the case of the financial set-up of the Navy which was to be delivered to Mr. Forrestal. The material prepared by the financial officers was so complicated, so technical that nobody could understand it, especially me. So eventually you would bring things down to fairly simple basics, take them, and more or less shake them down to what would be important to those listeners at that time in their particular climate and mood, and eliminate the things which they would not consider or which would not have a bearing on decision-making.

As a result I have been involved in something like 5,000 presentations in the last 30 or 40 years. I've never counted them, but they're up in that area and they are primarily presentations to management groups, not to sales groups or people like that. Usually they involved decision-making or communicating in some way, and as a result of the work that I did in the Navy when I was on active duty, over a period of time various ranking officers or Assistant Secretaries who had known of this work or had been told of this work called me to Washington to develop presentations and gradually I became a fairly regular consultant to the Navy at various levels.

One of the presentations on which I worked was the presentation made to the Eberstadt Committee at the time that there was a question as to whether the naval air force would be divorced from the Navy and put under the Air Force or whether it should be left under the Navy. I worked on that with the people who were concerned with it and was fortunate in having a successful presentation. I also worked on quite a few others at the CNO level, at the Secretariat level, at the fleet command level, and at the bureau level, such as the Bureau of Supplies and Accounts.

Most recently I have been working with Admiral McCain out in the Pacific when he was making up his presentations to the new Secretary of Defense, Mr. Laird, to Mr. Nixon when he came through, and to Agnew and so on, so that he could project to the President or Secretary those things which would be most important from the President's viewpoint, not that of the Commander-in-Chief, Pacific, or the Secretary's viewpoint, which is quite different from that of the military mind. And that is what I believe might be called my contribution, which was to translate a military viewpoint into the viewpoints and the pressures and so forth of a civilian official.

I have also been working fairly recently with Admiral Galantin when he was Chief of Naval Material, particularly on the subject of the overruns in contracts and what the true picture was and what might be done to prevent a recurrence of the thing. Incidentally, in that whole question of the overruns the image that the public and the services have of the entire situation is quite a false one, because although the overruns ran into something like a billion and a half dollars in money, out of something like 1,500 ships that were built in the shipbuilding program, the overrun applied to only 9, and they were very sophisticated ships like atomic carriers or missile-carrying cruisers and certain submarines that were entirely new types.

Q: It was a pioneering effort, then?

Mr. W.: It was a pioneering effort and the blame is not half as bad as it seems on the outside when Congress says, "Well, you ran over two billion dollars." Because over a third of that money had been authorized by Congress, and another third of the money was due to technological changes of which Congress was informed. So that the area of slippage - and there was an area of slippage in management - was a relatively small percentage of the total shipbuilding program.

Q: Yes. I want to ask you how did Secretary McNamara react to - ?

Mr. W.: Secretary McNamara wasn't there at the time. I think it was Secretary Laird, but I'm not sure. Mr. Chafee was

Secretary of the Navy at the time. I had one interview with him. I showed him some charts which I had worked out with Admiral Galantin which put a totally different aspect on this question of the culpability of the overruns because it wasn't as bad as it looked. In other presentations of that same general nature the trick, if you want to call it a trick, has been to sift out the important essentials from what is usually a mass of great detail, and very frequently it is the great detail that obscures the basic essentials.

So that has been my business for the last 20 years about.

Q: A very fascinating business!

Mr. W.: It's fairly unique.

During the course of my first consulting job with the Navy I gave a talked called "Presentation of Ideas," and Admiral Carney, who heard this talk, called me back to active duty toward the end of the Korean War and he asked if I would come down for a couple of weeks and give this talk to the deputy chiefs, the bureau chiefs, and the top brass in Washington. He said, "They will listen to you a little bit more politely if you put on your uniform because then you're not just some civilian professor trying to spout theories out."

So he put me into uniform and I was in uniform seven months and a half, and I gave that talk within the military establishment about 350 times. He asked me to put it into written form, which I did and got out a manual called <u>Presentation of Ideas</u>, which is now long out of print. But I believe that it had the largest circulation of any military manual of its time and, if I'm not mistaken, it ran 75,000 copies and was distributed to the various services.

Four years or five years ago I was asked by several clients simultaneously, one of whom was Admiral Raborn who was at that time Director of the Central Intelligence Agency, and also the then Assistant Secretary of the Navy, and several civilian clients if I wouldn't bring this talk up to date and put it into another manual. Because there was some confusion about who would break into the club, you might say, different people would say, "We'd like a piece of this," and somebody else would say, "That job fits into the thing." So one of the clients said, "Look, why don't you publish it on your own and we will buy enough copies to cover the cost and give you a fair profit." So that is what I did, and the first edition went almost entirely in large chunks, like 1,000 to Central Intelligence, 500 to one activity of the Navy Department - I think it was CNO's office, and 500 to Aerojet General, and International Minerals, and companies like that. The book has been reprinted twice since, but the job of running a publishing concern and doing my other work was more than I wanted to do, so I discontinued it. It's out of print now, although I still get orders about once a week for it, for copies of the book. It had fantastic distribution in the services. And that is called Effective Oral Presentation. That does carry my name as author. In Presentation of Ideas there is a note at the beginning saying "This is a condensation of a talk by Commander Watson given to various groups in the government" and so on.

It was *Presentation of Ideas* that got me into the Polaris program because Gordon Pehrson, who had heard my talk several times, was asked about a book that dealt with the subject of presentation. Admiral Raborn, when he started the Polaris program, which was then the Fleet Ballistic Missile Program for Jupiter, not Polaris at all, said "We are going to have a selling job to do and we've got to get some instruction on how to present our case." Mr. Pehrson said, "Well, there's a fellow named Watson who got out a book called *Presentation of Ideas*, which is the printed version of a talk he's been peddling around the military establishment and it's quite good. So why don't you get a bunch of copies of that book?"

Raborn was not that kind of a person. He said, "I don't want the book. I want the man. Where can I find him?"

I found out later that he had made, I think, 15 telephone calls before he finally reached me in the office of a client in Chicago. He said, in effect, "Next time you're in Washington, and I hope that's very soon, come down because I want to talk to you." Well, I was going to be in Washington the next week or so, so I met Admiral Raborn and promptly became his slave and disciple.

Q: The first time you met him?

Mr. W.: The first time I ever met him. He was the kind of person that I wanted to work for. On the very first day he said, I"d like to get our group together on this Fleet Ballistic Missile Program and I'd like to have you talk to them a little bit on the philosophy of what needs to be done to sell a program like this."

Q: His group was his advisory group?

Mr. W.: His group, his team. So he took me into a room and the entire team was sitting around a big table. I think there were probably 20, and that was the entire Fleet Ballistic Missile crew at that moment. So this was really the very beginning of the thing.

Raborn and I became very good friends. I still consider him a very close friend, and I worked with him and his various people for about eight years, throughout the inception of the program, and my job primarily was to develop the presentation and speeches that were necessary to get the program accepted, because at that time the Polaris program had about two friends. One of them was the Chief of Naval Operations and the other was the Secretary of the Navy. Nobody else wanted any part of it, because all the admirals felt this was a wild goose chase that was siphoning off money from their cruisers or their carriers or whatever their command needed money for, and this was just pure Rube Goldberg. But Raborn had a staunch ally in Admiral Burke and also in the Secretary of the Navy whose name I do not remember. It was not Mr. Matthews. I think it was the man who succeeded him.

Q: The Secretary was Tom Gates.

Mr. W.: Either Secretary or Under Secretary at that time. It was Mr. Gates.

I joined the program at the end of 1955 when it was very embryonic and it was still going to be the adaptation of the Jupiter missile to surface ships.

Q: That was at the point that Raborn joined it, wasn't it?

Mr. W.: That's right. He'd only been there a couple of months - three months at the most.

Then there was some question as to exactly where I would fit in from a technical standpoint, what would be my status. Finally, my status was that of a contractor. They made a contract with me to perform certain services at a certain rate to the degree that the Polaris company required those services and would inform me that they needed some services from me, then I would perform the services and bill them for the time.

Q: Something on the scale of Aerojet itself?

Mr. W.: Yes. I was a contractor. They had 20,000 contractors before they got through and I think I was the smallest contractor because I was one person. Anyway, that was an open-end contract which lasted for eight years, I believe, because, first, my job was to develop the presentation that was to be made to the service people themselves, who were highly critical, the congressional committees that were involved, to groups of businessmen, and even to contractors to explain to them what a ballistic missile was and where it would fit into the picture. Originally, they were going to mount these missiles on surface ships, cargo ships that were converted because they would have to be fired at the surface.

Q: That was in terms of the Jupiter?

Mr. W.: That was the Jupiter, which was a liquid-fueled missile.

Q: And huge in size?

Mr. W.: Yes, it was about the size of a pullman car. The trick was to set it on end and light it off on a surface ship and not blow up everybody in the vicinity, because they didn't have a nice distance where they could hide in cement blockhouses to watch the take-off.

Then they also had a bright idea of installing four missiles into a special submarine and the missiles would extend from the keel of the submarine right up into the sail, and those missiles would be fired on the surface. But more and more it became obvious that the liquid-fueled missile was not the answer. So a presentation was developed for President Eisenhower, I think in the late fall of 1956. Anyway, I had been connected with the program for less than a year and most of that time people were wringing their hands as to how they could fire this liquid-fueled missile from a ship and not blow up the ship too.

But by that time the research people felt that they had the answer to controlling the combustion of solid fuel, which had been the problem. It was no problem to set the thing off and make it burn. The problem was to control it, so that you could have these take-offs under control. And a presentation was made to President Eisenhower which said, in effect, "We, the Navy, are faced with making a recommendation to you for a decision. The decision is between having a missile which is not suited to launching at sea sooner, or to develop a missile which would be suited to launching at sea and having it later. So the question is simply one of time. We can develop a solid-fuel missile which can be fired from beneath the surface, from a submarine, which makes it a practically invulnerable weapon, if you will give us extra time for this development, because we do not think that any further money put into the liquid-fueled missile would be anything more than money down the rat hole because we just don't think it is a practical weapon."

Q: Did Raborn make that presentation to the President?

Mr. W.: Raborn did.

Q: Were you present?

Mr. W.: No. I never did anything by myself. I worked with

Raborn and various others, including Gordon Pehrson to shake this story down to a very simple executive decision, and Mr. Eisenhower's decision was quite typical. He said, "I want the good missile and I want it sooner." And he got it, because the original timetable was much longer than the final timetable.

Eisenhower simply said, "I want you to develop the missile in the same time frame as you were going to develop the Jupiter program and I know it's going to be quite a job to do." Raborn said, "We will do it."

Q: You had the same problem with Secretary Wilson, didn't you?

Mr. W.: I never had anything to do with Secretary Wilson, to be honest with you, because the presentations on which I worked went usually to the military or to congressional groups or to the President. They may have used the same ones on Mr. Wilson but I was not privy to that and I was not privy to Mr. Wilson's comments.

Q: Would you pause for a moment and elaborate on the preparation for the presentation to the President? How did you go about this? Did you use visual aids, or what did you do?

Mr. W.: Well, I'm going to go back one step farther, and that is that the speeches which Admiral Raborn made and the presentations which we developed at the beginning were streamlined down to answering three questions. The first of the questions was, would it work. The second of the questions is, when can we have it, and the third of the questions is, what would you do with it when we do have it.

So the presentations were structured along that line because the major obstacle always was the doubting Thomas who believed this was sheer Rube Goldberg and it wouldn't work anyway. If you could convince them that you had a missile weapon system that would work, then you got into the question of the time span, and finally you got into the question of how it would be used strategically or tactically as part of our defense structure. The presentations all followed that basic, simple outline. In fact, usually the first paragraph of Admiral Raborn's speech would run something like this:

> "I'm going to talk to you about the Fleet Ballistic Missile program," and he would describe briefly what a missile was, and then he said, "I'm going to talk in terms of the three questions that I have fired at me most frequently. The first one is will it work? The second one is when can we have it? And the third one is what will we do with it when we get it? I will develop each of those points."

So we always simplified it down to the kind of thing in which these people were interested. Anything else was subordinated to those three points because that was what we wanted to get over.

Now, in the case of the presentation to President Eisenhower, it was a visual presentation which I believe was put onto viewgraphs. We originally made it in panels, chart panels, 30 by 40, but I believe finally they were photographed into viewgraphs because the President wanted a somewhat larger audience to see this and the viewgraphs could be blown up. They discussed first what the need was, which, of course, was fairly obvious to the President but it was in terms of having a seaborne deterrent weapon and what could be done with it. Then we got into the question of the impracticability of the liquid-fuel missile and its limitations for strategic and tactical use, and the far greater desirability of having a missile that could be fired instantly and could be fired from beneath the water.

Of course, that sounded fine, but the President was going to ask a lot of very embarrassing questions. How will you communicate with the submarine? How can you provide guidance for the missile? What kind of construction would you have to have in the submarine? How can you have your navigation sufficiently pinpointed so that you know the point from which you're firing hoping to reach the point that you're aiming at? And all those questions were put into this presentation, as I remember it, along the line of "Mr. President, you naturally will want to ask some of these questions. The first one is so-and-so," and we went down the list.

Q: Anticipating?

Mr. W.: Oh, yes. In fact, the secret of a good presentation is that you anticipate what is in the person's mind and you answer it before he forms a question. So that, as I remember it, it wound up with the question of the timetable and the use of the thing, and left pretty much to the President's faith that the technical problems would be solved as we went along.

I remember one time he asked Admiral Raborn how the Navy Department or the President could communicate with a submarine under the water somewhere off the Arctic coast of Russia, and Admiral Raborn said, well, we haven't got it fixed yet but by the time the submarines are ready our communications system will be ready, and it was. That was pretty much the way the program was developed. We had to develop testing machines to test components that hadn't even been designed. Nobody knew how big the instruments were going to be and, as is well known, they cut a nuclear submarine in half and added, I think, 130 feet to the hull, and everything had to be compressed into that 130 feet. When they got all through some of the instruments had clearances of fractions of an inch because they had to fit into those things.

Incidentally, this is not known too generally but it might be to history that the reason that there are sixteen missiles in a submarine was a physical reason in that the control mechanism at that time could only extend the distance of four missiles. So they could have four missiles in two rows on one side of the machine and four missiles in two rows, or eight missiles, on the other side of the machine. That is what determined that there were sixteen missiles, rather than twenty or twelve or anything else.

That's all they could fire at the time of that particular design.

And they had a lot of other rather interesting things. They were going to fire the missile originally in a bubble of soap to cut down the friction as it went through the water, but they found it wasn't necessary. They made a great many experiments of things that eventually were jettisoned. For instance, they had, at the Jupiter stage of the program, what was called a ship's motion simulator, which was a very sensitive machine that would anticipate the roll and pitch of a ship and fire the missile at the exact instant that the tubes were vertical. Of course, that was scrapped because they were going to fire from under the surface and the thing wasn't necessary, but at the time they were going to fire this pullman car on its end off a surface ship and they had to be absolutely certain that it was vertical at the time of firing. The ship's motion simulator worked a little bit like a director in that it would not permit you to fire the missile until it was vertical. But they had to anticipate the roll and pitch of the ship by a certain fraction of a second so that it would catch the ship - catch the missile - vertical at the time that it would fire rather than at the time that you pressed the button.

There were a great many of those things that were extremely interesting.

Q: May I ask you a question? In the account in this book on Polaris and Admiral Raborn also emphasized the same point, that

when he made a presentation to Secretary Wilson, the telling
point was the cost and the amount that could be saved with the
solid-fuel missile over the Jupiter, and this is what convinced
Wilson to give the go-ahead. Did you include the subject of
costs in any of your presentations?

Mr. W.: Oh, yes. Every one of the presentations which was
developed was a tailor-made job in that it was aimed at the
audience to whom it was going to be delivered in terms of the
areas of their interest and possible participation. As, are you
trying to sell the program to somebody who will help boost it for
you? Or are you trying to sell the program to a congressional
committee that thinks of the money? Or are you trying to sell
the program to a military group that doesn't think the thing
will work anyway? Each presentation had to be pitched to the
particular audience to whom you were going to talk. And that
would change because, as the image of this project developed, the
emphasis in your presentation would change from trying to assure
these people that this Rube Goldberg thing really wasn't a wild
dream to assuring them that this was the best expenditure of
money that the country could make in the way of a deterrent, and
so forth.

There were strategical aspects of the presentation to
certain groups and money aspects to other groups. Some of the
most important presentations dealt with industry and showed how
the management was set up. If you know Gordon Pehrson, you know

about the PERT system, which I think is in that book.

Q: Yes.

Mr. W.: HE is a very large contributor to that. And some of the management things were Mr. Pehrson's. Some of the management things were Red Raborn's. He had almost as blank a check as you could get. But when it came to money, Admiral Raborn's position was - and he made this very clear in some of these presentations - that he could spend money only as fast as technical development permitted its expenditure wisely. For instance, if he had enough money to hire 5,000 nuclear scientists and put them on the pay roll at a high salary, there weren't 5,000 nuclear scientists available. You could not hire more than there were. And there were limitations all along the line. You couldn't possibly spend that money unless you had a product or a brain which could deliver what the money was to be spent for.

So there was a natural limitation on the expenditures, which was quite different from the congressional viewpoint of how much is this going to cost. In many cases Raborn's attitude, how much of this can I spend because what can I buy with it?

The money question was naturally of importance, but the technical development question was the one that really had people quite fired up in imagination because nobody had ever imagined sending a missile out of a submarine, shooting into the air nearly 3,000 statute miles, and having it hit a target the size of the Ile Fou, and traveling in the meantime at 10,000 miles an hour. That was just beyond people's imagination, including many of the people in the Navy.

Q: Mr. Watson, suppose we concentrate for a little while on the problem you had with Admiral Raborn in selling the idea of Polaris to the Navy itself? You said earlier that most naval officers were very skeptical about this Rube Goldberg project and really didn't want anything to do with it. Would you talk about that?

Mr. W.: That problem lived with us from the very first day that I was connected with the program, because the first presentation I ever saw was within two or three days and had been put together within the Navy, and it dealt a great deal with technical matters, but left out far too much of the question that here was a highly desirable goal to which no one could say no. In other words, strategically and tactically, here was a virtually invulnerable weapon system which had fantastic destructive power. I don't think there was one man in uniform who took the position that that wouldn't be a good thing to have.

Q: And, looming in the background, was there not a sense of urgency, we must do this?

Mr. W.: I'll come to that in a minute.

They would all agree that this was a desirable goal. Most of them would agree that, since the Sputnik affair had concentrated attention on the Russian missile program, there was an urgency there, and more than that, that we could not afford to be second rate in an entirely new era of weaponry. We couldn't afford to drag behind and we were behind now. There was an urgency, and that was a very important factor in selling this to the service. This is something we ought to have. If we can have it, it's wonderful, and we should have it just as soon as possible because the other fellows are developing it and they will have it and maybe we won't.

So it got down to the question of the engineering feasibility of it.

Q: That whole argument implies that it wasn't an impossible thing to do?

Mr. W.: Well, when we said the Russians are doing this, they've already sent things into space, it was not an impossibility. I think the most telling arguments, and Red Raborn or Gordon Pehrson may disagree with me on this, I think the most telling argument that we used was to convince them that this project was in the best possible hands and that the people who were working on the thing were the kind of people who got things done and could surmount these various obstacles. We had to sell faith in Raborn and his team, I think above almost everything else, because you can get into all kinds of arguments on technical points and no two engineers will agree, as no two doctors will agree and no two historians will agree on certain things.

But we had to establish that the team had been picked with utmost care and that they were people of accomplishment who knew their business, and that they were dedicated to this goal and we were going to lick these various obstacles as they came along.

Q: There were no doubts in this area, were there?

Mr. W.: The thing that seemed to get across to, you might say, the military skeptics was the quality of the team that was working on this thing to give them some confidence, because you could not give technical details at that time because they hadn't been developed yet. We didn't know what they were going to be. When the ship's inertial navigation system was developed, we weren't sure exactly what was going to come out of it. But it was developed by the best people they could find, and they put their noses on the grindstone and kept them at the job until these various things were licked one by one. And it is my own unofficial, but very deep, conviction that the success of a major presentation rests almost as much on the degree to which the presenters can inspire confidence as it does on the logic or facts themselves, because if you do not project a dedication and capability to your audience, no matter how good your facts are, there's always that lingering doubt in their minds.

I think that one of the greatest contributions to the program was Admiral Raborn's personal integrity and enthusiasm and common sense, and that you invariably felt that the thing is in good hands.

If anybody can do it, he can.

Q: Well, when he stepped into the job his reputation was an impeccable one, his qualifications were that, were they not?

Mr. W.: He was an aviator stepping into a submarine program. That griped some of the people. What's an aviator doing in submarines? There was a lot of little pecking and snapping at him. On more than one occasion I saw him when he came back from the Pentagon in a good Irish rage at some of the nit-pickers who were making his life miserable, and some of the nit-pickers were pretty high ranking nit-pickers. But many people just plain didn't think this could be done.

Q: I suppose it's always inevitable in the case of leadership that there's some effort to quash it.

Mr. W.: The interesting thing to me was the difference in the image of Admiral Raborn, who developed the Polaris missile, and his running mate Admiral Rickover, who developed the nuclear submarine. I believe those people who worked with Rickover worshipped the ground he walks on but, in general, his image has not been as favorable as that of many naval officers and he's considered a pretty tough customer. Whereas Admiral Raborn was just as tough a customer, but I never knew anybody who didn't like him in the Navy or out.

Q: He has the ability to relate to other people!

Mr. W.: He just had the ability to relate to his people. He could be very tough with them but they thought he was the greatest man alive, and my opinion is that he stands pretty high - he's well in the top segment of the people who have done most for this country, because he had a great many discouragements.

Q: How long did it take you to sell the idea to the Navy as a whole?

Mr. W.: You can't put a timetable on that. It was a progressive thing. The selling to the Navy and even to industry on the Jupiter concept ran into a great deal of opposition, as I remember it, and somewhat rightly so.

Q: I suppose that was a real deterrent to selling the other?

Mr. W.: It was a deterrent in one respect, in that a great many people - and some of them felt that they were fully qualified to believe that a liquid-fuel missile could not safely be installed in a ship and launched from a ship because of the mere job of preparing that missile for firing. You can't fire a liquid-fuel missile by just pressing one button. As you know, they have to fill up the liquid fuel. It takes quite a long time to get it ready and then it's a very delicate matter. So what they needed was an inert propellant which could be fired the way a shotgun can be fired or a rifle can be fired. And it is my recollection that the more the Jupiter looked impractical, the more the Polaris seemed to be the answer, and in some ways the Jupiter impracticability may have helped sell the Polaris because the contrast between the two weapon systems was so heavily loaded in favor of Polaris that, maybe, the idea of a missile - a fleet ballistic missile - could break some ground on the Jupiter concept. And, once it had broken ground for the concept, it was easier to move in with this specific weapon.

Now, I'm going to editorialize again for a minute, in that in my entire experience, which now covers roughly fifty years, in the field of selling ideas, you do not as a rule sell an idea all in one lump. It becomes a gradual process and people have to adjust to a change in concept about anything, and that is done over a period of time. It will be faster with some people, slower with others, immediate with a few, and never with others. But most people have to be conditioned over a period of time to accept a new idea of any kind. In fact, there is an author on the sea named William McFee - you may or may not have read some of his books. He was an engineer with the United Fruit Company for many years around World War I and he wrote very well. He became a writer by profession. But he was writing in one book that I have of the reception of the steam turbine versus the reciprocating engine by marine engineers, and he told about the resistance that the steam turbine encountered and he made this comment: one must never underestimate the enormous inertia of the human mind!

That was one of the problems that we had to lick.

Q: Well, you were aided and abetted by the fact that, once it got underway, the evolvement and the development of the Polaris itself was a selling point, wasn't it? I mean things were going along.

Mr. W.: Yes. Even the most rock-ribbed fleet admirals and so forth, I think, got their attention directed more and more onto the advantages of having this deterrent weapon and what could be done with it, as they gradually began to absorb the fact that maybe it could be developed because - there the Russians helped us a great deal because of the publicity on the Russian missile program, and that helped us along because it showed that missiles could be developed.

Q: How widespread was knowledge in the Navy of the work of Levering Smith in California with missiles earlier?

Mr. W.: Well, he had been doing the rockets, and I really have no idea. I know that some of the people in the missile program were brought in from the Talos and some of those other air-breathing missiles.

Q: Yes.

Mr. W.: But I believe the great breakthrough was the solid fuel business.

Q: Since you were close to Raborn and Burke, how did they feel about the Jupiter as a possibility? It had been forced on the Navy, had it not, but how did they feel about it?

Mr. W.: I couldn't tell you. I had no dealings with Burke at all on this program. I had dealings with Burke on other presentations. But as far as the Polaris program is concerned I never was in the same room with him on that program. I know that Raborn was very enthusiastic that an answer would be found to these various questions. He knew of the technical difficulties of the Jupiter missile and the dangers and so forth, but he was the kind of person who said, well, these are problems but there must be a way to lick 'em, so let's find a way to lick 'em. But I don't think he ever was too happy about the Jupiter program because so much of his mind was being occupied by the development of the solid-fuel missile, and that was really the answer. The other one was simply, as you say, something that had been sort of wished on him.

Q: In the development of your presentation, did you ever talk with those two young chaps?

Mr. W.: I'd like to make very plain that my own participation in this continuing program was not a continuous one and was only on a part-time basis. Certainly it was not the whole show, because all of these presentations were developed jointly with other people. There was always the Admiral, there was always Mr. Pehrson. There was usually the associate director of the project.

They had a succession of very capable officers in the grade of commander, such as Commander George Moran and several others whose names I don't recall, who did a lot of the day-to-day work in developing these presentations.

We had a graphics shop which was set up and finally had at least twenty people in it who helped prepare the graphics.

Q: Did you more or less supervise that shop?

Mr. W.: I was given a supervisory authority by Mr. Pehrson at first to get the thing going and had something to do with it, but that shop was used also for many of the internal presentations made by the various section chiefs to the Admiral or different units who had to make presentations on the status of the technical development of the program.

When it comes to the graphics, I think it might be of interest to mention that the Polaris project was the first major use on a continuing basis of a graphics system that I had developed, which showed a qualitative charting versus a quantative charting. That has been used quite widely in the government and in business ever since. But at that time only the office of the Chief of Naval Operations was using it occasionally, but on the Polaris system it was worked into the entire reporting procedure in the situation room so that the Admiral and others could evaluate programs at a glance or at least know how they were evaluated by the people in control.

Q: Would you illustrate that for me - the quantitative versus the qualitative?

Mr. W.: Well, it is a visual system and I can show you how it works. Basically, it grew out of two simultaneous meetings - at least they were within the same month. One was when Mr. Gordon Grey was Secretary of the Army he said that he had, at his various meetings, to follow protocol and go around the table in terms of the rank of the people sitting there. So he usually had to begin with a four-star general and by the time he got around to the one-star general who was connected with the specific problem that Mr. Grey wanted to go into, most of the time had been used up. So what he wanted was something that would sift out the things to which he and his group should obviously give their attention and concentrate on those things.

At about the same time Admiral Carney remarked that he had to keep abreast of a great many different projects and situations in a great many different fields. I think he gave the number 167. He said, "There are 167 things I'm supposed to keep track of, and when I come into the office in the morning there are half a dozen admirals and another half dozen captains in the waiting room, all of whom want to see me about some specific project which is close to their activity but which may not belong in the lap of the Chief of Naval Operations at all."

Q: And not be included in the 167?

Mr. W.: Exactly. So he said, "How can you visualise what I should devote my time to versus what I shouldn't?"

From those two conversations, a similar problem was exposed and a visual system was developed, as far as I know, it is unique, which interposes an opinion between the reporter and the reportee. In other words, the reporter has to evaluate the status of his situation in terms of what the reportee would want to know. In other words, it reverses the normal reporting process from developing what the person in charge of a certain section wants to tell the boss to what it is that the boss wants to know.

Q: And needs to?

Mr. W.: Yes. Primarily it's a change in viewpoint, so that the person doing the reporting must evaluate the status of that subject, and it is the evaluation that is reported and not the statistics and the numbers.

Now, the question, of course, always is how good is the evaluation?

Q: Yes, this calls for gray matter!

Mr. W.: And there is a good deal of resistance to this program in the lower grades, because each man has to go on record as to where a thing stands, but that is exactly what the boss wants to know. He doesn't want to be given a bunch of papers and told, now you figure out what this means. He wants, here is the situation and it's status is good or unsatisfactory or in danger or something like that.

The principle of it was very simple. I can show you the way the thing is done graphically, but basically each situation is evaluated on one of five levels: very good, satisfactory, marginal, unsatisfactory, or critical. You can't evaluate them in between those five levels, but the simple way to do it is to evaluate them in those five terms, and Admiral Raborn, with his gift for expressing things in words, said it's very simple and this is the way I want these things scored. If I knew as much as John JOnes does about his particular project and felt that John Jones should get a pat on the back from the Admiral or have a medal pinned on him because it's in such good shape, I want you to put it at the top, very good. If it is in a status where John Jones feels that he has it under control and that the Admiral doesn't have to worry his pretty red head about it, unless for some reason he wants to ask about it, he can erase it from his mind. Then it should be on the 'satisfactory' level. If, on the other hand, John Jones feels that for some reason the Admiral might want to look into it because there are either present or future problems that he might want to know about, he puts it in the 'marginal' level so that the Admiral can then make up his mind whether or not he wants to look into that situation on that day, or earmark it to look into later.

"Now, if John Jones feels that he needs some help in licking the problem, he puts it in 'unsatisfactory,' but when he puts it down in 'critical,' it simply means, 'Admiral, you've got to get some help to lick this problem."

That's the way Admiral Raborn expressed it and that is the way we ran the thing for I don't know how many years, but I think it's still in use. The criterion for making these evaluations was, again in Admiral Raborn's language, "I want the best-qualified guesser to give me his best guess as to where this thing stands today because certainly the best-qualified guesser is a better guesser than I am obviously. He knows more about it. Then I want to get an honest guess on the thing, and I'm going to judge my officers to the degree that they reflect the situation truthfully and accurately and not the degree to which they might think they could impress me with how well they are doing, because if I ever find somebody who says a thing's in very good shape and I find it isn't in very good shape and he just wants to cover up something, I'm going to have his hide."

Q: This implies he expected top efficiency from his men at all times?

Mr. W.: This implies that each man at each level should make an evaluation of the status of the thing that was under his charge in terms of the way the boss would want to have it because he wants to know if it is good or bad, and not whether somebody's going to hope that it will come out all right. He wants to know what the real situation is.

At first, there was a little resistance to it but eventually the thing worked out very satisfactorily because you had an evaluation at every level. Let's take a certain project of which an evaluation has to be made, and the first evaluator is a lieutenant. He then evaluates it to his boss, who is, let's say, a commander. And the commander says, "Well, now, why do you say that this is satisfactory when such and such might be the case." And they talk it over and they will come to an agreement that it should be at that level or maybe a level a little higher or a level a little lower. Anyway, it's checked at the next level. So, by the time it gets up to the Admiral, it has been checked at each operational level and they will come to a consensus.

It is almost impossible that a situation that is really critical will be evaluated as "very good." The areas of difference are above or below the marginal level, or just below satisfactory, or a little bit above unsatisfactory. They are small variations of grade. They are not the blacks and whites. But even those small variations of grade are of greatest use to the boss because what he wants to know is where should I put my time today? This will work for money, performance, quality, inspection, public relations - anything at all in the same visual pattern, because the level is simply translated into what it is, a unit of time, or a unit of money, or a unit of performance, or whatever else it may be, state of completion, whatever it may be. A situation is good or bad in its own terms and that's what the boss wants to know.

Q: How frequently did he want to know this?

Mr. W.: Well, there were two ways of doing it. Both were used.

One of them was a lot of things at the same time. Let's say, the first of the month, or every two weeks. And the other one was a thing over a period of time, such as you have an evaulation, let's say, twice a month of a program and you can see whether it is moving up in peformance or moving down or isn't moving up rapidly, or has it leveled off. You can follow its motion and you can do it at a glance.

Q: You were telling me, off tape, some time ago that you spent only about seventh days a year -

Mr. W.: I was supposed to give one day a week, which is fifty days in the year, to the Polaris program, some of which time was spent in Washington at the headquarters of the project and the rest of the time was spent at home preparing material or writing speeches or brochures and things of that sort. I believe that the largest unit of time in the program was seventy days in one of the years, but I don't remember which year. I was supposed to give them fifty days and it climbed up into the seventies in one year.

Later, when I was getting out this Polaris book, it ran into a good deal of time over a fairly short span of months, and I gave quite a lot of time to the project for a period of, say, three months.

Q: How did the presentations, which were very numerous in industry and elsewhere in the country, run? Was there a strenuous effort at the beginning of the Polaris program, and did it taper off, or was it a continuous thing?

Mr. W.: No, it was continuous.

Q: Would you talk about the preparation for congressional presentations and how frequent were they?

Mr. W.: I don't remember how frequent they were. I know that we worked on several of them, and in most cases the material presented to congressional groups was a combination of elements which had been presented to other groups. Usually there was a little bit more emphasis on the money factor and the timetable, rather than on the technical things. I cannot remember but one or two presentations that were developed especially and solely for congressional groups.

Usually Admiral Raborn had to make the presentation and we put together elements that would be of interest to that group at that time and used the same visuals.

Q: Was there an organized effort with the news media?

Mr. W.: Oh, yes.

Q: How was that accomplished?

Mr. W.: It was handled through the public affairs officers.

Q: The Navy Department's public relations officers?

Mr. W.: No, the Polaris public relations officers. In fact, we had a broadcast through CBS on the program once, which was put on television, and that was something that they worked on for quite some time.

Q: Was that a kind of a documentary?

Mr. W.: Well, it was the Polaris program. There were interviews with Raborn and Pehrson, and it showed test runs and things like that, building, shots, and things of that nature. It was a very good show. I think it was a full hour. And then Raborn was on "Meet the Press," and programs like that from time to time. He was called upon to make Veterans Day speeches. I don't know how many speeches he made and I don't know how many I worked on with him, but none of them was the work of one man. It was all a team effort.

Q: What about newspaper editors?

Mr. W.: They had a program, yes, to meet them and they brought them in quite frequently. Quite a few times when I was working in the office there, Commander Moran or whoever was the public relations man would bring in editors or writers and people of that profession to get publicity for the program. The program was a natural as far as its glamor was concerned. Many of these people really wanted information, and information kits were developed and distributed to these people and to visitors to the plant and things of that sort.

Q: How was this very remarkable spirit engendered? Was it through the presentations, through the speeches, and so forth?

Mr. W.: Admiral Raborn's personality and enthusiasm and dedication to the thing. He had a very magnetic way of speaking. But the subject itself was so dramatic, so staggering, that it was a natural for write-ups and interviews and things of that kind, because there were relatively few news stories in the same league with the idea of shooting a missile from way below the surface of the ocean into a target nearly 3,000 miles away and having it hit that target with more destructive effect than I don't know how many bombers would represent. In fact I believe that we used to claim that a Polaris submarine carried more destructive force than all offensive armament of all wars in all history. That used to be challenged, but the margin was sufficiently high so that there was no doubt about it.

Q: Now, was this all an element in engendering of enthusiasm for the project? This was a time of peace, and we had been through the Korean War, which again was not a very popular war and people were fed up with it and this was one reason why the General was able to do what he did in terminating it, but here we were dealing with an instrument of war and we were talking in terms of ability to destroy. Was this at all a factor in publicizing it?

Mr. W.: It was a factor, as I remember it, particularly in view of the fact that we had lost our monopoly of atomic weapons and were now sharing that weapon with the Russians. So we could be on the receiving end of an atom bomb as well as on the sending end, and I think that really is what scarved the bejeebers out of the people. They knew of the destructive power of the bomb from Hiroshima and Nagasaki and the publicity it had and Bikini and so forth, but at that time we were the ones who had the weapon and the victim was the other side. But when Russia got the atomic bomb we could easily be the victim. So there was a lot of attention given to the deterrent effect of a weapon which, as we said - from which, as we said, an aggressor could never escape because sooner or later it could wipe him off the map because it didn't have to be fired immediately the Russians attacked us. We didn't have to retaliate with the Polaris at that minute. The Polaris submarines could be hanging around the south pole at the time, but they could get up there and they would plaster their targets eventually because nobody could stop them.

I think that was the thing that really did the job. The country was a little bit scared and they were particularly scared at the Sputnik, which seems a long time ago.

Q: I remember it very vividly, the reaction nationally and internationally.

I wonder if you would turn your attention now to the great effort which was made with industry. You said, at one point, they were over 20,000 contracts let by the government.

Mr. W.: There were 20,000 contractors, as I remember it. Well,

I'm not qualified to speak the way Mr. Pehrson could speak, or certainly the way Red Raborn could speak of the industrial setup, but in general that, too, was a team operation in that different major contractors had slices of the program which they worked on through their subcontractors, and then there was an assembly contract which I think was Aero Jet, or it may have been Lockheed. I think it was Lockheed.

Q: They built a special plant.

Mr. W.: Yes, they built a special plant to assemble these missiles. But there were a great many very unusual problems dealing with industry and the inventiveness of industry. For instance, how were we going to transport these missiles from one place to another? How were we going to load them into the submarines? They had to develop special cranes, special mother ships, tenders. They had to develop testing devices because the first few tests were not successful, as you may remember. They had to nurse this thing all the way along with a great many intangibles still in existence. The fire control and guidance, the navigational problem with the ship's inertial navigation system. They never at the start were quite sure just exactly what its place would be, how much space it would take up, and how it would perform, but that was one of the great successes.

Communication was another great success, as to how they could keep in touch with their submarines. But a very interesting thing in which industry was also involved was the solving of some of the human problems that were inherent in a situation that was virtually unheard of, of sending roughly a hundred men below the surface of the sea who would never see anything for two months. It was not "Join the Navy and see the world," but "Join the Navy and keep out of sight." So that the environmental problems - they had various organizations with whom they worked to work out some of these things - temperature, even a uniform that wouldn't pick up any lint, all kinds of things like that. How did they dispose of garbage? How did the toilets work under that pressure for that length of time, because these ships were not coming up to the surface like normal operating submarines? They were going to stay down below.

They had to work out the question of material outlasting human facilities, which of course has been given much publicity. But there's one little story that might be of interest because I was involved in that in a slight way.

They decided that each submarine should have two crews. That is like having a woman have two husbands, and it was contrary to all naval thinking, and when first proposed to Admiral Burke I understand he roared out, "What are you going to have? A crew of boys and a crew of girls?"

The facts of the matter were that you could not subject a single crew to the routine of the Polaris operation. So you'd have to have two crews and eventually the Navy swallowed that innovation, but there came into the picture a rather delicate problem as to who would be senior to whom. Should they have an A crew and a B crew? Or a first crew or a second crew, or an X crew and a Y? What were they going to call these two crews, which on the face of it had to be absolutely equal in status and everything else? You couldn't have a first team and a second team.

As you know, the Navy colors are blue and gold. Well, it so happens that I went to a prep school which was Choate and its colors were blue and gold, and they had intramural sports as well as the varsity sports, so the school was divided into the "blues" and the "golds," and you were automatically assigned to one of the other color when you joined the school. So there was no question of choosing sides. Boy A would be a blue, and Boy B would be a gold, and Boy C would be a blue again, and so forth. They were merely taken in the order in which they were registered in the school.

Q: And at a time when their potential wasn't known?

Mr. W.: Absolutely. There was no question of superior choices or anything like that.

So I suggested that since the Navy colors were blue and gold, why didn't we call the crews blues and golds because there was no particular preference in the Navy colors between the gold and the blue. It was just the blue and gold of the Navy, even though the blue on a sweater might have more area, the gold was a little bit more -

Q: It was mentioned first!

Mr. W.: Yes, it can be gold and blue. It doesn't make any difference, but that was adopted and the blues and the golds - I believe the captains flipped a coin to see which would be the blue captain and which would be the gold captain, because they wanted to keep it on an absolutely equal basis and not put it on the seniority of the skippers, because the skippers changed. But the blue crew stays the blue crew no matter who's skipper and the gold crew stays the gold crew no matter who's skipper.

That was something for the Navy to swallow because, as you know, in any formation you trail along. If you happen to be the junior skipper you get all the dirty jobs to do.

I thought that might be of a little interest.

Q: Indeed, yes.

Mr. W.: I don't know how many people know that this was the result of the Choate system, because I don't even remember just who the people were who were at the meeting. But at that time the blue and gold had not been thought of. Since that time, I've heard much rationalization of the blues and the golds as being the Navy colors, but I don't think at that time anybody had thought of using colors.

Q: The presentations to industry were so terribly effective. Did you have a major role in preparing some of these speeches and, if so, how did you draw upon your own personal knowledge of industry in selling and so forth?

Mr. W.: Answer Number One, I cannot claim a major role in these things because they were all team operations and they were tailored to the particular problem, and different people were brought in for different problems. For instance, I know the group that might make a presentation to the Electric Boat Company people might be quite different from one that would address the Businessmen's Club of Omaha, Nebraska.

Q: Were you useful to them in pointing out the differences that there were and the need for careful selection in the team?

Mr. W.: Let's put it this way. Admiral Raborn or Gordon Pehrson, our deputy, would say, "The Admiral's going to make a speech in Omaha, Nebraska, to the Businessmen's Club. Will you throw together the material that you think would fit that kind of an audience?" which would be quite different from the material that would be thrown together to talk to a group of electrical engineers of underwater laboratories. In many cases, I didn't have enough technical knowledge to be of any use at all on the technical side, but sometimes helped put together these things in collaboration with the technicians so that the main story did not get lost in the details. That was the biggest problem I had. It was the biggest problem in the weekly presentations made to the Admiral because the charts were loaded with too much detail and there were usually too many charts. I fought a valiant but losing battle to keep the charts simple and few in number. That's a war I never won.

Q: But the mere fact that you kept at it was important!

Mr. W.: I'll put it this way. Mr. Pehrson's resume some years later when he saw some things on the Polaris said, "I could still find a few fingers of Watson's fine Italian hand in some of the charts"!

Q: Tell me, Sir, how you used certain elements of this story judiciously. The pioneering aspect in terms of industry, testing things that hadn't yet been invented and that sort of thing. The impediments which seemed insuperable. How did you use these elements?

Mr. W.: As far as industry was concerned, as I remember it, the theme was here is a true emergency and crisis, we've got a problem that's got to be solved and we can't solve it by ourselves. Everybody has got to get into the act with their expertise and so forth and help us solve it. We found that people preparing food, for instance, worked out later that compressing these foods into volume which would permit the submarine to carry two months' food supplies. A turkey is a pretty big, bulky piece of cargo, but by the time they had finished de-boning it and compressing it and so forth, it took very little space. Even problems like that had to be worked out with industry, and there were all kinds of industries. I've mentioned already clothing and food and bedding, I remember. Amusements, such things as exercise devices, movie screens and movie films that would take up as little space as possible. Taped courses for college education so that the men would have something to learn. The selection of the books. All of those things were worked out with specialists in the field and, as I remember it, they were eagerly cooperative to try to lick this problem because they realized the ramifications of a problem like this.

Q: Then that pushes it back to the publicity that was attendant upon it. I mean getting these people to realize this was true!

Mr. W.: That's right. I would put it this way. At the beginning you had to tell them what a ballistic missile was and we compared it to a base ball, in that a baseball gets its entire velocity from the arm and fingers of the pitcher, and once it leaves the hand of the pitcher it is on its own and it operates by the laws of physics, its resistance, trajectory, and everything like that. Once it's left the pitcher's hand, there's nothing you can do about it to change its course. Unlike a rocket, which propels itself, or a jet engine which propels itself all the way along, this missile was thrown by a gigantic pitcher's arm and the trick was to have it pass through an exact spot at an exact speed on an exact course, so that the laws of physics would determine its trajectory and land it in the right spot, because once it has left the propelling charge it was on its own and there was nothing that you could do to it, except to intercept it somewhere, because you couldn't change its course.

Q: Who dreamed up that graphic metaphor?

Mr. W.: Of the pitcher? I cannot truthfully say who did, but I know that I used it at one meeting, but maybe fifteen other people had used the same analogy. I don't know, but I do remember writing that for one speech and the people there thought it was a good analogy but I'm quite certain that that was such an obvious analogy that a lot of other people used it, too.

That was the first thing we had to explain - what a ballistic missile is versus a rocket or projectile or anything like that. Then we had to develop the fact that the Russians were building these things - that the Russians had a missile program - so we had to have a defensive operation. So there was that urgency involved, and one of the easiest things on the urgency question was that General Eisenhower, President Eisenhower, had given the ballistic-missile program as high a priority as anything could have with the Atlas, the Titan, the Polaris, and so on. They had very high priority. So there was a lot of publicity on missiles and on priority and on the urgent need for it, and every time the Russians sent somebody into outer space winging around the earth, why, it gave it another push because it showed that these things could be done, and I think that helped us a lot.

The intriguing thing about Polaris was firing this thing from beneath the sea, from a position that nobody could see to a target that the firing unit couldn't see. The fellow who fired was hidden and as far as he was concerned the target was hidden because he couldn't see it, either.

Q: But he could determine the target, he knew where the target was, whereas the enemy couldn't determine him?

Mr. W.: That's right.

Q: His location?

Mr. W.: That's right. We used a lot of very simple things which dramatized us to the public. We were talking about the final missile, which was the 2,500-nautical-mile missile. I think it was called the A-3. And when you talked about being able to hit any part of the world's largest land mass, we used that, and there was no place on earth which was too far from the sea to be hit by this missile, but we used a simple example.

For instance, you could take a Polaris submarine and sail it out to sea out of sight of New York, submerge it, fire your missile, and land it in what would be a large football stadium out of sight of land to the west of San Francisco, if they had such a football field built out there in the ocean. It would cross the entire continent in about twenty minutes.

There was a rather amusing situation on that because I had

put that in the book that I wrote on the Polaris program called *Adventure in Partnership*. And in London the operational people were talking about the range of the Polaris missile, and I used this example and said we could fire it from about fifty miles east of New York and hit a target fifty miles west of San Francisco. They said, you're crazy, you're nuts, the missile can only make 2,500 miles and it's nearly 3,000 miles from New York to San Francisco. So I said, "Well, you look it up." They argued about that so I went and got a copy of this book which was in Admiral McCain's office there and I read the paragraph out of the book, and I said, "There it is. It's in the book." And the chief intelligence officer said, "Who the hell wrote that book?" I said, "I did." Then I reminded them that 2,500 nautical miles are about 2,870, or something like that, statute miles and the crow-flight distance from New York to San Francisco is just under 2,800 miles!

Q: So they were pacified!

Mr. W.: That was one of the few moments that you have on a thing like this! Who the hell wrote the book. I did!

Q: Well, now, your presentations had to vary in terms of depth also. I mean, when you were presenting the story to the naval officer you had to be technical, when you were presenting it to the populace at large, it had to be somewhat emotional, did it not?

Mr. W.: On that, I'd like to draw a distinction among naval officers, having had a good deal of experience in writing advertizing copy for engineers, for doctors, and for specialists of one kind or another. I learned long ago that the less technical you make your copy and the more you appeal to their common sense and emotions, the more successful it is, because you can never be quite as technical as they think they are. They're always picking holes in your technical stuff, but people react to emotions. We found that we could write medical copy to certain persons in very simple language, which was much more effective than using all the medical and surgical terms, because the minute you start using those they can disagree with a term that you're using or something like that. If you keep your eye on the ball of what you're trying to sell, you're better off. So, as I remember it, in many of these presentations, we avoided getting too technical and laid the emphasis on the emotional thing, the urgency of the situation, the value of the missile when we had it and what we could do with it, and things of that sort, because you could never satisfy them on the technical details anyway. Furthermore, no two technical men ever agreed in advance on anything, as far as I can remember!

That is not maligning the technical people but, as doctors or any other specialists, they had different ideas and interpretations, and if you kept out of those controversial areas you were better off.

Q: Would you talk about the departmentalization in industry which seems to have been such a successful expedient for the Polaris program? I mean Lockheed building a special plant dealing only with Polaris, other industries with contracts having a wing of the factory where they put all the workers involved in Polaris.

Mr. W.: I don't think I could talk intelligently on that because it's something I had virtually nothing to do with. You use the term "presentations" so freely, but actually once you were on that team you did almost anything that came along. It was not that sharply divided. I got into all kinds of projects which had relatively little to do with presentations.

Q: For instance?

Mr. W.: For instance, firing the head of the graphics shop. I was brought into that one.

Q: Well, of course, that did have something to do with presentations and proper presentation!

Mr. W.: As a matter of fact, what it had to do with was the personality of a person. There were a lot of things that you got mixed up in.

I had to make a presentation on the Polaris program at the Bureau of Ships' basin - the David Watson Taylor Model Basin. I was talking to a group that had arrived there for some kind of a meeting and I found out afterwards that they were the very highest level of scientists and nuclear experts and God knows what else - sort of the Einsteins of the country - and I was telling them about the Polaris missile. Well, inasmuch as I didn't know much about the technical side of it, I harped as much as possible on the urgency of the situation, the ingenuity of the team in meeting these problems, gave some examples of how the various problems were being met, and I have never had a more receptive audience. And all of these people were highly experienced and trained technicians of one kind or another. I suppose if I'd gotten into the technical aspects of the Polaris they'd have scorned me!

Q: At least humiliated you!

I was thinking also of something Admiral Raborn told me, again generating this tremendous spirit and the idea of getting the personnel in a factory together on a Saturday morning together with their wives and their children -

Mr. W.: Oh, yes, they did that.

Q: - and talking to them.

Mr. W.: And then they had a big recruiting program for the crews of these ships, because that was a wholly new concept - burying yourself for two months - and that was worked out on a human basis so that the sequence of duty would ensure that a man would be home every second Christmas, for instance. He could plan on this, and he would know when he was going to be away and when he was going to be at home. They thought that there might be friction between the crews. But, as I remember it, the gold crew that is operating the submarine under the water leaves its families sort of in charge of the blue crew and they look after them like big brothers. It has worked out very, very well. In fact, in view of the racial troubles the Navy's having now, I have made some trips on Polaris submarines and there was absolutely no racial discrimination whatever, and we had people of all colors. Some of the men of a darker color were among the most respected technicians on the ship. As far as I know, they had no trouble there at all.

Q: This is the objective that Admiral Zumwalt is driving at.

Mr. W.: Yes.

Q: And it's been achieved in Polaris.

Mr. W.: As far as I know. Remember I have't had any direct contact with the program for quite some time, but the last time I was out in a Polaris submarine the man who gave me the best explanation of how a certain piece of very complex equipment worked was a colored man, a very bright fellow. He was a first class petty officer, and he was greatly respected. I think the man who explained something else to me was a chief petty officer, who was also a black man. You couldn't see that there was any problem there at all. It may have changed.

As a matter of fact, I made a trip in the carrier Essex about four or five years ago and they had quite a few black men in the crew and there was no problem there. They got along with the white ones fine. So this may be different from what I remember.

But in picking the crews they went through a lot of psychological study, and the interesting thing was it took longer to train the crew than it did to build the submarine. They'd assemble the crew and start training them before the keel was laid.

Q: Then they had to have some assurance of re-enlistment and what have you, did they not?

Mr. W.: I suppose so. I don't know. I'd rather not give an opinion on that because the whole question of recruiting and training of personnel was in the hands of some extremely capable officers whom I greatly admired. In their way they were just as ingenious in solving some of these problems as the people who developed the communications system or the garbage-control system or whatever else it might be.

There's one thing I would like to emphasize in relation to both publicity and presentation methods and things of that nature, in that when Admiral Galantin relieved Admiral Raborn there was absolutely no slackening in either the interest that the Admiral took in that facet of the job or the support that he gave to it. Except for the difference in personalities, you never would know there had been a change at the top, because Admiral Galantin gave me just as much support and encouragement as Admiral Raborn ever had. And although he's a different personality, he's a person I respect equally. He's also a good, warm, close friend of mine. In fact, he was here a couple of weeks ago and spent the day with us.

So the feeling at the top, their relations with the public, industry, the other services, and within the Navy, was always kept very prominently as a major element of the Polaris program.

Q: It never slackened in that sense?

Mr. W.: Never slackened, as far as I can remember.

Q: As you got toward the end of the project and your period of association with it, did your duties change any?

Mr. W.: Yes. The last year my job was primarily getting out this book Adventure in Partnership.

Q: Who wanted that out?

Mr. W.: I did. I say that unblushingly because I felt that after a cruise many ships get out a cruise book, high schools get out a year book, college classes get out a year book as a souvenir for the people who took part. And I felt that the Polaris program should have a year book which should be given to the people who had made the program possible.

So I made up a dummy which was not too unlike the final book and showed it to Admiral Raborn, and he thought it was a good idea, and he said, "Now, the people who are going to pay for this are the major contractors who have had these big contracts."

Then Admiral Raborn was relieved and a few weeks later I showed the dummy to Admiral Galantin and he said, "Why, certainly, we want to go ahead with this." So he invited me to come down to the Naval Academy on a certain morning when the leading contractors were all to be there at a meeting. He said, "I will give you the first half of a coffee break to present your proposal to these people and see what they say."

It happened to be the morning after the Thresher was lost, and I think the Superintendent was a submariner, Galantin was a submariner, and there were quite a few other submariners there who had very long faces. It was not a cheerful morning for the submarine contingent or for the Navy as a whole.

Q: It was a bad time to go on, wasn't it?

Mr. W.: But they had this coffee break and I showed to these people, of whom there were ten, the dummy outline of what it would be. It would be a book that any layman could understand, it would be largely a picture book, but it would tell the story in human and not technical terms, and would be given to the people who had made the Polaris program possible, and that includes secretaries and clerks and messenger boys and other people on the program, not just the admirals.

Well, at the end of about three minutes Dan Kimball, who was president of Aero Jet said, "What are we wasting time for? Let's go ahead and do it and not take any more of our time. Do we all agree?" They all agreed.

Then Kimball said, "Why do you only want to print 20,000 copies? Why not print another 20,000 copies and give it to every high-school library in the country, or the best high-school libraries?" So they all agreed to that, and that was the entire presentation. They all sent me the checks and I went ahead, gathered the photographs, and painfully and laboriously wrote each chapter to be chopped to pieces by the technical advisors! But eventually we came to a happy meeting ground between telling the story in sufficiently technical terms to be believable, but also in simple enough terms that anybody could understand it.

That is how the book grew.

So for the last six months, I would say, most of the time I spent was going around to the contractors, collecting the money, getting their pictures, getting their stories, persuading them to accept my layout and copy, and all but one of them did, helping Admiral Burke with his speech, working on Admiral Raborn's speech with him, and Admiral Galantin's speech with him, and putting the book together.

Q: In the way of a comment, I can see what school of public relations you belong to! I looked in vain for the name of the author at the beginning of the book where it normally is and I couldn't find it. I do find it at the very end in a kind of a footnote, the concept of the book itself, its layout, selection of illustrations, text, and so forth is the work of Commander Clement Hayes Watson.

Mr. W.: That's right. I'll tell you the reason for that. There was a very delicate question as to who should be given personal recognition by name, and you didn't know where to start. Should you just take the director, the associate director? Should you take all the heads of the various components, such as launching and handling, solid fuel, and so on? But where do you stop on a program like that?

So we agreed that no names would be mentioned at all beyond that of the Chief of Naval Operations, who would write the foreword, Admiral Raborn, who would write his speel as director of the project, and Admiral Galantin, who would write his speel as successor to Admiral Raborn. And at the very end Admiral Galantin looked at the proofs and said, "Tom, your name isn't in here anywhere."

I said, "No, we decided not to put names in."

He said, "All right, we're going to put it at the back of the book saying that you are the person responsible for this book because I think we owe it to you."

And that is how the book came out.

Q: I'm glad to have that explanation because it's not exactly normal with a book.

Mr. W.: If you look at my other book, you'll see the name on the cover!

Q: Yes. Tell me, in connection with the preparation of the book, a great deal had been written and publicized on Polaris, and yet certain aspects of the missile are still classified. Did you have any problem with that in selecting the pictures and other things?

Mr. W.: Number One, I had no problem on the technical side of it because I wouldn't understand the classified technical details anyway! Number Two, on pictures, yes, I had some problems. I went through over 4,000 pictures to make the selection that is in this book. We picked out the pictures for their pictorial value, for the clarity with which they illustrated, for their human nature value, and for the fact that they would not show anything classified. But I had to go to every contractor individually and go through his picture file, I had to go through the Navy Public Relations Office or the Polaris picture files. I even took some pictures myself because we needed some to fit in here and there. I don't remember now just which ones I took myself.

Oh, I went also to the news services to get pictures of the launchings and things of that sort.

You will notice that it is dedicated to the three presidents, and in the case of Mr. Johnson, he had made no comment whatever about the Polaris since he was president. This was put out shortly after Johnson took office because the proofs were in final form when Kennedy was shot. So we found a couple of quotations from Mr. Johnson as Vice President and we put them in there, but we did not say that it was President Johnson who had said these things. We had to weesel around that a little bit!

We set aside 500 copies to go to VIPs, and by VIPs I don't mean just presidents or Mrs. Johnson or Mrs. Kennedy or senators and so on, but people like Nehru, Prince Philip, de Gaulle, leaders of different countries, and the reason for that was because they felt that this concept of an Adventue in Partnership was a tremendous plug for the free enterprise system, and they wanted to publicize the partnership that had existed between the military, the world of science, and the world of industry-

That's why those books were sent out so freely with personal letters from Admiral Galantin or from the President, as a matter of fact. President Eisenhower sent out some and so did President Johnson. Admiral Galantin had a very thick book containing the acknowledgments from all of these VIPs. You name 'em and they're in there. I don't think anybody failed to acknowledge it.

Q: Then there was some reflection of what you had hoped to achieve?

Mr. W; Yes.

Q: In terms of here is free enterprise in operation?

Mr. W.: Yes, and I think we sent Nehru something like 25 copies for his Cabinet or something like that. I know we sent them to foreign countries with particular emphasis on what free enterprise could do if it really wanted to. I think we sent them to Russia. as a matter of fact.

Q: Why not!

Mr. W.: I don't know, but, as I say, Galantin has a great big book of acknowledgments, which he showed me once. It has the most amazing cross section of prominent people. Mrs. Kennedy wrote a beautiful letter thanking us for dedicating it partly to her husband.

Q: For your edification, Admiral Raborn told me that this was, in his opinion, the only satisfactory portrayal of the story in print.

Mr. W: I'm glad it is because it was written entirely to a layman. I even let my wife read chapters of the thing to see if she could understand it. I'll tell you a rather amusing story.

One of the divisional captains, the head of a division, I think it was launching and handling but I'm not certain, was given the chapter that I had written to check and edit to make certain that the statements were correct, and he sent back a blistering memorandum to the Admiral which began: "I am quite unable to understand how you could ever permit anything as puerile and childish and stupid as this thing ever to appear in print. For example, this person said they were going to launch the missile in a bubble of soap. Ridiculous." And he mentioned a number of other things. Utterly ridiculous. Never heard of anything like that. He said, "That person had better check on his facts a little bit. Second, his use of English would cause a high-school teacher to burst into tears. I suggest that maybe he might benefit from a course at Harvard. Finally, it's perfectly obvious that the person who wrote this has never had much to do with the Navy."

Pete handed me this letter, smiling, and said, "Let's write him an answer." He thanked the captain for his comments and said, "Now, as far as the facts are concerned, as to the bubble business, this was instigated at such and such a time and abandoned at such and such." He took every one of those things that had happened before this man came into the picture, and he said, "Insofar as the Navy is concerned, the man who wrote this was in the Navy long before anybody who presently is on active duty was in the Navy and has been in the Navy through three wars. Furthermore, you talk about the high school teacher and a Harvard education, this man taught English composition at the school to which John F. Kennedy went and he also is a member of the Harvard class of 1920 in good standing"!

I thought that was a rather amusing thing, but it was so wonderful. We never had any more comment from that captain.

But, in general, the divisional officers were very cooperative. I had long talked with quite a few of them and got their assistance to make sure that we got the guts of what we were trying to say and could express it in terms which were both interesting and understandable, and if you will notice at the front end [format] of the book you will find the advertising man sticking out because every chapter has a headline and subhead, like an advertisement!

And that is rather rare in books. I don't know if you'd noted that or not.

Q: Mr. Watson, would you say a few words about the team aspect of this whole Polaris project? It was such a tremendous accomplishment. Admiral Raborn has emphasized and stressed the fact that so many people were involved in it, "It is a team," said he.

Mr. W.: He has always treated the whole subject from the team standpoint, from the very first day I met him when his first invitation was phrased, "I want you to come and meet the members of our team." He didn't say "my team," he said "our team." He got a great deal of personal publicity because he's a colorful person and he was the spearhead, but I think he always leaned over backwards in accepting that accolade as a personal achievement because he always brought his people in, particularly people like Gordon Pehrson, Levering Smith, and so forth.

In fact, on one occasion he was asked who would be the one indispensable man in the program, and he said, "Levering Smith, barring none, including me." So I think Admiral Raborn subordinated his own contribution far more so than many people would, and emphasized that this was a team product, and before he bawled anybody out, I think he gave them several pep talks on being a member of the team. I think the only times he ever bawled anybody out was when somebody fell down on him, and of course he could do it very nicely. But in the allocation of jobs and duties I never had the feeling that I had just this little niche, because if I wanted to make a comment on anything I did it and they would listen to it, or I would be put onto something else for a while and chase around on some errands in connection with the program because it was that kind of an operation.

Q: Did you attend some of those staff team sessions on Saturdays?

Mr. W.: Oh, yes.

Q: Tell me how they were conducted.

Mr. W.: They usually took a basic subject and the man in charge of that particular operation would just get up and make a presentation, and I would writhe in my seat because he usually was much too long and much too detailed and frequently, I felt, was confusing the audience. But, then, making simple presentations is supposedly my business and it used to grate me to see the great detail into which these people went which I felt was an unnecessary use of the time of all of the people there. IF he wanted to take the Admiral's time and the Admiral wanted to go into that much detail, that was a matter between the Admiral and himself, but when there are thirty or forty officers sitting there through material devoted to a very small facet of the operation and from the looks on their faces it was exceedingly boring to some of the people. I felt that those meetings could have been sharpened up a lot.

One thing that contributed very markedly to the esprit de corps was the Admiral's insistence that all of his officers and enlisted personnel wear their uniforms all the time they were on duty in the special projects office, because at that time there was a wave of getting into civilian clothes and hiding your identity as a naval officer and so forth, because civilian clothes were permitted. Raborn took the position that this was a military operation and it was a military team, and he said, "I think we ought to wear our military uniforms when we're playing in this game." I think that had a great deal to do with the esprit because you saw the people coming in every morning and they were in their uniforms, and I'm all for that.

You take the opposite case, in the public information office you hardly ever saw anybody in uniform and it was a much sloppier run outfit than Polaris. In Polaris the offices were neat, the enlisted men stood at attention, and you had a military sense, which you did not have when you got into the Pentagon.

Q: It seemed to go with the sense of urgency!

Mr. W.: Yes, it was a military operation. It was a campaign, and I think in civilian clothes it would not have had the impact, the esprit de corps, of having people wear their uniforms.

Q: That's a very interesting point, and I believe the idea was carried out in industry where, in some places, they did wear special uniforms or badges or something of the sort.

Mr. W.: They had a little sort of a tie clasp thing - they had these submarine tie clasps, yes. I have a couple of those. I don't remember that they had a special uniform. They may have later. At the beginning, no.

Q: As a wind-up to your tour of duty with Polaris, you told me off tape that you visited all the plants that were involved in the Polaris production.

Mr. W.: No. I visited all the plants that contributed to the publishing of this book, and I did that for two reasons. One was to get their stories as best I could and get pictures from them, and the other one was to get approval on the layout and text that I had prepared. Usually I made the layouts first and I told them the text as I got information from them, and then I fitted pictures into the layout as best I could.

Q: Here, as we look at this book, is an illustration of what we were talking about. At Hughes Aircraft the girls in their gay red, white, and blue Polaris blouses.

Mr. W.: Incidentally, on the back cover is a lovely picture. I don't know if you noticed it.

Q: Yes, I did.

www.ingramcontent.com/pod-product-compliance
Lightning Source LLC
Chambersburg PA
CBHW082150070526

44585CB00020B/2155